n keeping your statutes! Then I shall not be put to shame, having my eyes fix
ents. I will praise you with an upright heart, when I learn your righteous r
statutes; do not utterly forsake me! How can a young man keep his way pure
it according to your word. With my whole heart I seek you; let me not wande
ents! I have stored up your word in my heart, that I might not sin against
O Lord; teach me your statutes! With my lips I declare all the rules of you
f your testimonies I delight as much as in all riches. I will meditate on your
s on your ways. I will delight in your statutes; I will not forget your word.
with your servant, that I may live and keep your word. Open my eyes, tha
things out of your law. I am a sojourner on the earth; hide not your comman
soul is consumed with longing for your rules at all times. You rebuke the in
wander from your commandments. Take away from me scorn and contempt, for
monies. Even though princes sit plotting against me, your servant will meditate
four testimonies are my delight; they are my counselors. My soul clings to
ording to your word! When I told of my ways, you answered me; teach me
e understand the way of your precepts, and I will meditate on your wondrous w
away for sorrow; strengthen me according to your word! Put false ways fa
iously teach me your law! I have chosen the way of faithfulness; I set your
g to your testimonies, O Lord; let me not be put to shame! I will run in the w
ents when you enlarge my heart! Teach me, O Lord, the way of your statute
he end. Give me understanding, that I may keep your law and observe it with
d me in the path of your commandments, for I delight in it. Incline my heart t
, and not to selfish gain! Turn my eyes from looking at worthless things; an
ays. Confirm to your servant your promise, that you may be feared. Turn a

tes day and night. He is like a tree planted by streams of water that yields its fruit in, and its leaf does not wither. In all that he does, he prospers. he wicked are not so, that the wind drives away. Therefore the wicked will not stand in the judgment nor ngregation of the righteous; for the Lord knows the way of the righteous, but the wa d will perish. Psalm 1 "Blessed is the man who walks not in the counsel of the w in the way of sinners, nor sits in the seat of scoffers; but his delight is in the law and on his law he meditates day and night. He is like a tree planted by streams of w its fruit in its season, and its leaf does not wither. In all that he does, he prospers. ot so, but are like chaff that the wind drives away. Therefore the wicked will not stan ent nor sinners in the congregation of the righteous; for the Lord knows the way of ous, but the way of the wicked will perish. Psalm 1 "Blessed is the man who walk el of the wicked, nor stands in the way of sinners, nor sits in the seat of scoffers; bu t is in the law of the Lord, and on his law he meditates day and night. He is like a reams of water that yields its fruit in its season, and its leaf does not wither. In all t ospers. he wicked are not so, but are like chaff that the wind drives away. Therefore ot stand in the judgment nor sinners in the congregation of the righteous; for the Lor of the righteous, but the way of the wicked will perish. Psalm 1 "Blessed is the mar not in the counsel of the wicked, nor stands in the way of sinners, nor sits in the se rs; but his delight is in the law of the Lord, and on his law he meditates day and nig tree planted by streams of water that yields its fruit in its season, and its leaf does n that he does, he prospers. he wicked are not so, but are like chaff that the wind driv fore the wicked will not stand in the judgment nor sinners in the congregation of the r e Lord knows the way of the righteous, but the way of the wicked will perish. Psal ssed is the man who walks not in the counsel of the wicked, nor stands in the way of sits in the seat of scoffers; but his delight is in the law of the Lord, and on his law nd night. He is like a tree planted by streams of water that yields its fruit in its seas

CHOOSING THE ONE THING

THAT MATTERS

WOMEN'S GUIDED

BIBLE STUDY JOURNAL

Copyright © 2022

First Edition

Brooke Hamlin & Colleen Butler

Copyright © 2022 by Brooke Hamlin All rights reserved.

No part of this publication may be reproduced, stored or transmitted in any form or by any means, electronic, mechanical, photocopying, recording, scanning, or otherwise without written permission from the publisher. It is illegal to copy this book, post it to a website, or distribute it by any other means without permission. First edition

The website addresses and books recommended throughout this book are offered as a resource to you. These resources are not intended in any way to be or imply an endorsement on the part of Brooke Hamlin, or the Good Portion books, nor do we vouch for their content. All brand names and product names used in this book are trade names, service marks, trademarks and registered trademarks of their respective owners. The publishers and this book are not associated with any product or vendor mentioned in this book. None of the companies or products referenced within the book have endorsed the book.

Unless otherwise indicated all Scripture quotations are from the ESV® Bible (The Holy Bible, English Standard Version®), Copyright © 2001 by Crossway, a publishing ministry of Good News Publishers. Used by permission. All rights reserved." Scripture quotations marked (NIV) are taken from the Holy Bible, New International Version®, NIV®. Copyright © 1973, 1978, 1984, 2011 by Biblica, Inc.™ Used by permission of Zondervan. All rights reserved worldwide. www.zondervan.com The "NIV" and "New International Version" are trademarks registered in the United States Patent and Trademark Office by Biblica, Inc.™ Scripture quotations marked (NLT) are taken from the Holy Bible, New Living Translation, copyright ©1996, 2004, 2015 by Tyndale House Foundation. Used by permission of Tyndale House Publishers, Carol Stream, Illinois 60188. All rights reserved.

ISBN: 9781737259350

Text by Brooke Hamlin

Original Illustrations by Colleen Butler and Brooke Hamlin

TO OUR MOTHER/GRANDMOTHER MARTHA,
THE "MARY-EST" PERSON WE EVER MET.
THANK YOU FOR TEACHING US TO
CHOOSE THE "ONE THING" THAT TRULY MATTERS.
THE AROMA OF THE LIFE YOU POURED OUT FOR
CHRIST IS STILL TEACHING THE WORLD
WHAT LOVE LOOKS LIKE.

THE BEST ADVICE I CAN GIVE YOU:

LOOK UNTO JESUS,

BEHOLDING HIS BEAUTY

IN THE WRITTEN WORD

-Isaac Newton

Table Of Contents

1) INTRODUCTION — 12

2) EVERY WOMAN'S BATTLE — 18

3) SEE THE BIGGER STORY — 28

4) INVITATION TO INTIMACY — 38

5) INTIMACY BEGINS WITH INFORMATION — 44

6) INTIMACY REQUIRES INTENTIONALITY — 48

7) INTIMACY IS IGNITED THROUGH OBEDIENCE — 52

8) ROMANCING THE MIND — 62

9) WHY DOES PROCESS MATTER? — 71

10) HOW TO STUDY YOUR BIBLE — 77

11) BLANK JOURNAL PAGES — 111

12) PERSONAL REFLECTION AND GROUP STUDY QUESTIONS — 172

13) MEMORY VERSE CARDS — 183

14) RESOURCE PAGE — 192

...eady you are clean because of the word that I have spoken to you. 4 Abide in me, ... the branch cannot bear fruit by itself, unless it abides in the vine, neither can you, ... in me. 5 I am the vine; you are the branches. Whoever abides in me and I in hi... ...ears much fruit, for apart from me you can do nothing. 6 If anyone does not abide i... ...n away like a branch and withers; and the branches are gathered, thrown into the ... ...d. 7 If you abide in me, and my words abide in you, ask whatever you wish, and ... ...ou. 8 By this my Father is glorified, that you bear much fruit and so prove to be ... ...s the Father has loved me, so have I loved you. Abide in my love." If you keep ... ...andments, you will abide in my love, just as I have kept my Father's commandmen... ...s love. 11 These things I have spoken to you, that my joy may be in you, and that y... ..." This is my commandment, that you love one another as I have loved you. 13 Gr... ...o one than this, that someone lay down his life for his friends. 14 You are my frie... ...I command you. 15 No longer do I call you servants,[a] for the servant does not ... ...aster is doing; but I have called you friends, for all that I have heard from my ... ...made known to you. 16 You did not choose me, but I chose you and appointed you th... ...d bear fruit and that your fruit should abide, so that whatever you ask the Father ... ...ay give it to you. 17 These things I command you, so that you will love one another. ... ...the true vine, and my Father is the vinedresser. 2 Every branch in me that does ... ...he takes away, and every branch that does bear fruit he prunes, that it may bear m... ...eady you are clean because of the word that I have spoken to you. 4 Abide in me, ...the branch cannot bear fruit by itself, unless it abides in the vine, neither can you, ...in me. 5 I am the vine; you are the branches. Whoever abides in me and I in hi... ...ears much fruit, for apart from me you can do nothing. 6 If anyone does not abide i... ...n away like a branch and withers; and the branches are gathered, thrown into the ... ...d. 7 If you abide in me, and my words abide in you, ask whatever you wish, and ...

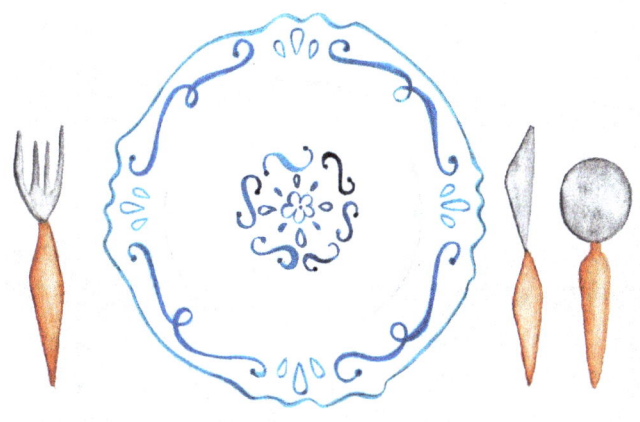

HUNGRY?

Introduction

What would happen if you only ate one meal a week?

Perhaps you're like my husband and can go long periods of time without food and not even notice. I am repeatedly shocked when he announces that he "forgot" to eat lunch. In my experience, "forgot" and "food" don't belong in the same sentence. I can barely make it between breakfast and mid-morning snack!

Though we all tolerate fasting differently, no one could survive on only one meal a week. Our bodies were designed to function on consistent, solid nutrition. *Food is our fuel.* On the days my husband neglects to eat, he usually comes down with what he refers to as, "the shakes" by dinner. His fingers tremble as he scours the kitchen for the nearest snack to scarf down or sweet tea to chug. He may be able to go the better part of a day without the effects of hunger, but if he tries to go much longer — *he notices.*

Why does this matter?

A recent survey shows that only one-third of churchgoers read their Bible on a daily basis. (1) Many Christians choose to feed their souls on the Truth of God's word only once a week during corporate worship. Here's the scary part — many of us have been depriving our souls for so long that *we don't even notice we're starving.*

We have gotten used to walking around with a permanent case of the "soul shakes," and have accepted a malnourished and atrophied spirit as the norm. Some of us have never known anything life could feel any different.

This statistic reminds me of my eight-year-old self. I was extremely near-sighted as a child. When I use the word, "extremely," I mean my parents discovered the extent of the problem when they asked me to read a giant road sign, and I replied in complete sincerity, "What sign?!"

Before you give my family a hard time for not noticing my handicap, I had never once complained about my lack of vision. I had been living in a fuzzy, color-drained world for so long that I thought, *"This is just what life looks like."*

When I tried on my first pair of glasses, I stumbled over backward in shock. I didn't know you were supposed to be able to see individual leaves on trees or the expressions on others' faces from across the room. The beauty of lacy-pink cherry blossoms and the reassuring smile of a friend had always been there, waiting to be enjoyed, *I just hadn't been able to see it.*

When we choose to forgo the nourishment of scripture, we miss out on the beauty of "the abundant life" that Christ came to offer us (John 10:10). We are content with living half soul-starved and stumbling around in the dark. Some of us have been living without the clarity and the energy that the Word provides for so long, that we have fooled ourselves into thinking, *"This is just what life looks like."*

CHRISTIANS FEED ON SCRIPTURE. HOLY SCRIPTURE NURTURES THE HOLY COMMUNITY AS FOOD NURTURES THE HUMAN BODY. CHRISTIANS DON'T SIMPLY LEARN OR STUDY OR USE SCRIPTURE; WE ASSIMILATE IT, TAKE IT INTO OUR LIVES IN SUCH A WAY THAT IT GETS METABOLIZED INTO ACTS OF LOVE, CUPS OF COLD WATER, MISSIONS INTO ALL THE WORLD... HANDS RAISED IN ADORATION OF THE FATHER, FEET WASHED IN COMPANY WITH THE SON.

-Eugene Peterson

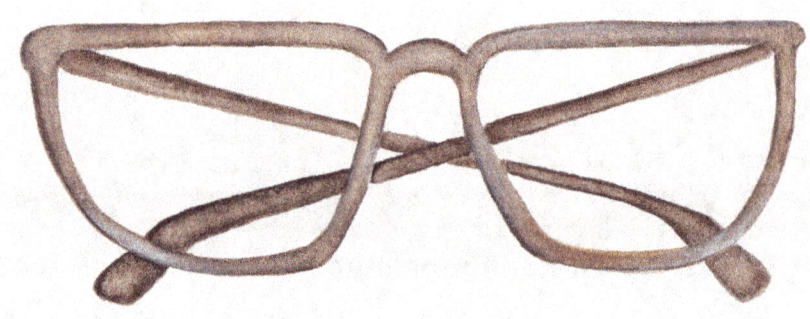

"EATING" THE BIBLE ON A DAILY BASIS IS LIKE PUTTING ON A NEW PAIR OF GLASSES.

Christ had something better in mind for His followers. He said, "I am the light of the world. Whoever follows me will not walk in darkness, but will have the light of life" (John 8:12). The Psalmist calls the counsel of the Bible, "A lamp to my feet and a light to my path" (Psalm 119:105). God has prepared a feast for us in His Word: promises dripping with affection, encouragement layered in love, the unparalleled delights of His Person served up for our enjoyment.

When the Jewish people talk about studying Scripture, they don't use language like "reading" the Bible, they talk about *eating* it.(2) They refer to their daily Bible study as their "parashah," meaning "portion."(3) Through this imagery, they recognize that the Word of God is the one essential they need to sustain them throughout their day.

"Eating" the Bible regularly is like putting on a new pair of glasses. We are able to see the world as it really is — the danger of darkness' deceptive allure, the joy and triumph of a soul set free, the beauty of God on display in even the smallest created things.

One of my prayers for the "Good Portion" study, is that it would reawaken a hunger in the heart of women for the Word of God. I want us to take "eating" the Bible as seriously as we take eating chocolate. (I take eating chocolate VERY, VERY seriously. Not gonna lie, I already ate two pieces of it after my dinner and am now considering leaving my computer to get a third.)

Maybe you've buried your craving for Christ under the stress of a rigorous work schedule and chauffeuring children to twenty different sporting events. Maybe you recognize your desperate need for spiritual food, but you have a toddler attached to each leg and can't remember the last time you had a moment to yourself. Or maybe you've been dining on the Word for so long that you feel Truth has lost its flavor. You have been faithful to come to the table of Scripture but have forgotten how to enjoy the Bread of Life.

This journal was written to give you the tools you need to become a proficient "self-feeder." We want to hand you the "fork" and "knife" you need to properly dissect and ingest the sweet nectar of the Word for yourself. We want to teach you how to slow down and savor each bite, allowing it to nourish and strengthen you. We want to help you find your rhythm for ingesting Truth on a daily basis, rather than having to wait for a once-a-week binge at church.

This study process was designed to be useful for the seasoned divider of Truth, the new believer, or the person who has never cracked open the pages of a Bible. You don't have to be an expert in theology to glean from Scripture. If you are in Christ, He has placed His Spirit in you to help you both understand and live out the truths He has given us in His Word.

We just have to come humble, and come hungry.

Mary has chosen the good portion, which will not be taken away from her. Luke 10:42 but one thing is necessary. Mary has chosen the good portion, which will not be taken away from her. Luke 10:42 but one thing is necessary. Mary has chosen the good portion, which will not be taken away from her. Luke 10:42 but one thing is necessary. Mary has chosen the good portion, which will not be taken away from her. Luke 10:42 but one thing is necessary. Mary has chosen the good portion, which will not be taken away from her. Luke 10:42 but one thing is necessary. Mary has chosen the good portion, which will not be taken away from her. Luke 10:42 but one thing is necessary. Mary has chosen the good portion, which will not be taken away from her. Luke 10:42 but one thing is necessary. Mary has chosen the good portion, which will not be taken away from her. Luke 10:42 but one thing is necessary. Mary has chosen the good portion, which will not be taken away from her. Luke 10:42 but one thing is necessary. Mary has chosen the good portion, which will not be taken away from her. Luke 10:42 but one thing is necessary. Mary has chosen the good portion, which will not be taken away from her. Luke 10:42 but one thing is necessary. Mary has chosen the good portion, which will not be taken away from her. Luke 10:42 but one thing is necessary. Mary has chosen the good portion, which will not be taken away from her. Luke 10:42 but one thing is necessary. Mary has chosen the good portion, which will not be taken away from her. Luke 10:42 but one thing is necessary. Mary has chosen the good portion, which will not be taken away from her. Luke 10:42 but one thing is necessary. Mary has chosen the good portion, which will not be taken away from her.

SHE DID WHAT SHE COULD.

-Jesus of Nazareth

Every Woman's Battle

Does any of this sound familiar?

"I will not hit snooze, I will not hit snooze!" you groan as your fingers fumble for your phone in the dark. You feel quite proud of yourself as you slip out of bed and attempt to slink silently to the kitchen. As you empty out yesterday's coffee grounds you tell yourself that this will be the day — you *will* read your Bible. As you begin filling the pot with water, you hear a soft whimpering sound and realize your toddler has awakened early. Your shoulders slump in defeat as you mentally calculate how much alone time a sippy cup of milk and some cartoons will buy you. As you plop him in his comfy chair and the sounds of *Cocomelon* fill the air, you notice your husband's muddy work boots are sitting in the middle of the living room floor.

Trying not to be annoyed, you drag the boots to their spot by the door, trailing clods of dirt across the carpet as you go. You tell yourself you will clean up the mess later as you head back into the kitchen and are startled by your big kid, who has also awoken early. "Momma, I can't find any socks," he complains. You are about to ask him why needs sock at 6:00 a.m. when his lower lip trembles and his eyes fill with tears, "My feet are cold," he whimpers.

You sigh and walk into the laundry room. As you sort through the sock basket, you notice the blinking red light on the washing machine and realize you never switched last night's load over to the dryer. Panicking, you remember it's game day and your son's shirt is still inside. You sit the coffee pot on a shelf and begin haphazardly emptying out the dryer before hefting armloads of wet clothes inside. You sniff the sleeve of a damp shirt and shrug, "It will have to do."

Your son meets you with a questioning look as you head back to the kitchen. "My socks?" he says. "Oh, right!" you spin around and toss one Batman sock and one Christmas sock from the mismatched pile in his direction, "Go watch tv with your brother."

"But I'm hungry," he protests. In one swift motion, you snatch the entire container of granola bars from the top shelf and drop it into his hands. "Juice box in the fridge," you add before he can ask for a drink. You march to the bookshelf and grab your Bible before you face any more distractions. As you head to finally finish brewing your coffee you hear your big boy shout, "Momma, did you give the baby chocolate for breakfast?"

Sensing something is awry, you bolt into the living room to discover your toddler plucking small brown bits out of the carpet and shoving them into his open mouth. You shriek and snatch him from the floor, swatting the hardened, boot mud from his fingers. He wails as you tote him to the bathroom and you spend the next few minutes picking tiny pieces of gravel from his gums and cheeks.

As you return to the kitchen, you strap the baby in his highchair and pour a larger than usual helping of puffs onto his tray. It takes a minute of searching before you remember you left the coffee pot in the middle of the living room floor. Your stress begins to melt away the moment you push the "grind" button and hear the comforting whir of the blades creating your long-awaited cup of morning glory. You lean in close and take a long, deep whiff of the sweet aroma, hoping to absorb some caffeine from the air.

While you wait for it to finish brewing, you slide into your seat and push your Bible onto the table before you. You decide you have missed the window for any formal reading plan and let the heavy book flop open by itself.

"Habbukuk," you read, bending over the pages.

"What's a *Habb-u-kuk*?"

Deciding your brain is not quite up for the challenge of deciphering this foreign-sounding word, you flip back a few pages and find yourself in "Nahum."

"That's better," you smile, "At least I can kind of say it."

Now let's see. Your eyes land on chapter 3, verse 17.

> "Your princes are like grasshoppers,
> Your scribes like clouds of locusts
> Settling on the fences in a day of cold —
> When the sun rises, they fly away;
> No one knows where they are."

You furrow your brow and run your fingers through your hair. *Could their princes jump really high? Are Israeli insects nocturnal?* You shake your head and decide to check on the coffee.

As you rise from your seat, your husband appears from down the hall wearing workout clothes. He has his EarPods in and is singing softly to himself. He doesn't seem to notice you as he bee bops himself over to the coffee maker, grabs your favorite mug and fills it to the brim. You stare in strained, shocked silence at the now-empty pot, and realize you will have to wait for it to refill.

"Oh, good morning, honey!" He gives you a smile and a quick kiss, "Figured I'd hit the gym early today with the guys."

You continue to stare open-mouthed as he shovels sugar and cream into the cup before taking a large swig,

"Oh, that's good coffee," he sighs.

"MEN MAY WORK FROM SUN TO SUN
BUT A WOMAN'S WORK IS NEVER DONE."

"Daddy!" Your big boy stumbles into the room and throws himself around your husband's legs. It's an adorable sight and you don't even react when half of the coffee sloshes from your husband's mug and onto the floor. You numbly grab a paper towel and toss it onto the mess before lumbering back to your seat before your open Bible.

Let's see, where was I? *Ah, yes.*

"Settling on fences in the day of cold…"

You feel a gentle squeeze on your shoulder as your husband leans over you. "Look at you, Miss Overachiever!" He croons, "Doing a Bible study!"

You chuckle softly, "Yeah, well, I'm trying."

"What'd you learn about?!"

"Well," you mutter, "just about some locusts…that like to…*sit on fences*."

"Oh," he says.

"But only when it's cold…and only at night," you add.

"Oh, that's nice honey," he pats your shoulder, "I want to hear more about it later." He kisses the top of your head before pedaling toward the door, "Love you! Proud of you!" He calls over his shoulder.

"Love you too!!" You shout back, and you mean it. You love this crazy, messy, beautiful life of yours, but you are beginning to wonder if meaningful time with God is possible at this point.

Maybe your kids are grown and gone, but you have a to-do list that's as demanding as a two-year-old child.

Maybe you have a work schedule so intense that when you arrive home, you have just enough energy remaining to melt into the couch and reach for the remote control.

Or maybe a scene like the one described happened in your house this morning. These events are loosely based on a recent day in my sister's life in which it took her 45 minutes to make a cup of coffee. I am only able to sit down at my computer right now because my children are currently curled up in little "nests" they have made themselves out of laundry baskets and have been "hatching" creatures out of eggs (balloons) all morning.

Whatever season of life in which you find yourself, the woman's battle to carve out time for personal Bible study is intense. Women don't get to "clock out." We arrive home to find that our work is still waiting there for us.

There's an old English proverb that says,

>"Men may work from sun to sun,
>But a woman's work is never done."

I would like to stop and clarify that I am not here to complain about my duties as a wife and mom. I love my life and was just thinking how gloriously grateful I am for the wonder of helping to provide a safe place for my family to grow and thrive.

I am also not here to disparage or belittle men. We need men. The world desperately needs more men acting like men. I happen to be deeply in love with one of them. He's a six-foot-two southerner with an adorable smile, and we've been happily married for over eight years now. I am so grateful for his godly leadership of our family and his faithful support as I pursue my Kingdom calling.

I simply desire to demonstrate that the woman's struggle to find alone time with God is typically different than the struggle that faces our men. A friend recently shared a Facebook post that highlighted this distinction and God's faithful response. The author explained that we don't find the Bible chocked-full of examples of women escaping to the mountains to meet with God. What we do find, is a God who comes to meet with women "right where they are." (1)

"He meets them at the wells,
Where they draw water for their families,
In their homes,
In their kitchens
In their gardens.

He comes to them
As they sit beside sickbeds,
As they give birth,
Care for the elderly...

Even at the empty tomb,
Mary was the first to witness Christ's resurrection,
She was there because she was doing the womanly chore of properly
preparing Christ's body for burial.

In these seemingly mundane
And ordinary tasks,
These women of the scriptures found themselves
Face to face with divinity." (2)

We created the "The Good Portion" because we wanted to give busy women a practical tool to get the most out of the time they spend in the Word. Please know there is no one "right" way to study the Bible. God has wired each of us to process information differently. Ultimately, it's up to the work of the Holy Spirit to produce any real inspiration and lasting change in our lives. This does not opt us out of the responsibility of regularly engaging with and submitting to the Word.

With this in mind, we want you to know that there will be days where doing an hour-long quiet time will simply not be possible. It is my prayer that we would all grow to be a little more like the woman who anointed Jesus at Bethany. She surprised the disciples by crashing a dinner party and cracking open a bottle of expensive perfume on the feet of Christ (Mark 14:3-9).

Though some disciples criticized her for spending her wealth in this way, when profits from the perfume could have been used to benefit the poor, Christ shushed their protests and said, "She has done a beautiful thing for Me," and that, "Wherever the Gospel is proclaimed in the whole world, what she has done will be told in memory of her" (Mark 14: 6,9).

To me, the most intriguing part of this passage is the reason Christ gave for calling her gift, "beautiful."

He didn't say this was the most expensive gift He had ever been given.

He didn't say that the smell of the perfume was exceptionally fantastic, or that she was an exceptionally attractive woman.

He said that the whole world would remember her sacrifice simply because, "She did what she could" (Mark 14:8, NIV). Not, "She did more than anyone else ever had," but that she did what *she* could. The eyes of all of human history are on this woman because she took what she had to give, and *she chose to give it to Jesus.*

Sister, God sees you. He sees your unique battle to create some space just to be with Him. He knows there is always something else to be done, always some task beckoning at the corner of your mind, always a stray sock, an overflowing basket, a hungry stomach that vies for your attention.

We can always find a different way to spend the valuable commodity of our time other than to pause and pour it out at the feet of Jesus.

Let it be said of us that we "did what we could," to give Him the best that we have. Don't waste your time worrying over what others can do, or what you are unable to do.

Give Him what you can.

Just because you were only able to battle out fifteen minutes today, don't believe the lie that this investment isn't beautiful in the eyes of God. The story of this woman's sacrifice was one Christ wanted told again and again. We're doing it right now!!

I want Jesus to cherish the way I used my time today. I want it to echo off the halls of Heaven. I want it to be a memory He replays over and over in His heart.

When Mary anointed the feet of Christ in John 12, the author included an uncharacteristic bit of sensory detail. He said, "The house was filled with the fragrance of the perfume" (John 12:3b). When we give what we can, it is not only a beautiful thing in the eyes of God, it creates beauty in your home. The scent of your renewed spirit after meeting with the living God will permeate and change the atmosphere of your house, your neighborhood, your church —whoever you encounter will taste the sweet scent of a life poured out for Jesus.

I WANNA TAKE MY PASSION

AND PUT IT IN A BOTTLE

JUST TO BREAK IT AT YOUR FEET

I WANNA TAKE MY AFFECTIONS

PUT THEM IN A BOTTLE

JUST TO WASTE THEM AT YOUR FEET

-Misty Edwards

The war to spend time with Christ is the one thing in your life that's worth fighting for, and worth winning.

Jesus told Mary that the time she chose to spend sitting at His feet and listening was, "The Good Portion, the one thing that wouldn't be taken from her."(3)

Let's learn to sort through the mess and choose the Good Portion.

y, and there was no longer any sea. I saw the Holy City, the new Jerusalem, comi
aven from God, prepared as a bride beautifully dressed for her husband. And I h
e from the throne saying, "Look! God's dwelling place is now among the people, and h
them. They will be his people, and God himself will be with them and be their God.
every tear from their eyes. There will be no more death' or mourning or crying or
rder of things has passed away." He who was seated on the throne said, "I am mak
ything new!" Then he said, "Write this down, for these words are trustworthy and
to me: "It is done. I am the Alpha and the Omega, the Beginning and the End.
ill give water without cost from the spring of the water of life. Those who are victori
rit all this, and I will be their God and they will be my children. But the cowardly,
lieving, the vile, the murderers, the sexually immoral, those who practice magic arts, t
all liars—they will be consigned to the fiery lake of burning sulfur. This is the secor
velation 21:1-8 NIV I did not see a temple in the city, because the Lord God Alm
Lamb are its temple. The city does not need the sun or the moon to shine on it, for the g
d gives it light, and the Lamb is its lamp. The nations will walk by its light, and the
n will bring their splendor into it. On no day will its gates ever be shut, for there wi
t there. The glory and honor of the nations will be brought into it. Nothing impure
y it, nor will anyone who does what is shameful or deceitful, but only those whose name
ten in the Lamb's book of life. The angel said to me, "These words are trustworthy a
d, the God who inspires the prophets, sent his angel to show his servants the things
take place." "Look, I am coming soon! Blessed is the one who keeps the words of t
ten in this scroll." Revelation 22:1-7 "Look, I am coming soon! My reward is wi
give to each person according to what they have done. 13 I am the Alpha and the O
st and the Last, the Beginning and the End. Blessed are those who wash their ro
may have the right to the tree of life and may go through the gates into the city. 15 O
dogs, those who practice magic arts, the sexually immoral, the murderers, the idolaters
yone who loves and practices falsehood. I, Jesus, have sent my angel to give you a

EVERYTHING SAD WILL COME UNTRUE

-- Sally-Lloyd Jones

See The Bigger Story

Imagine your high school English teacher assigns you a book report on the novel of your choice. The catch -- You must construct the entire report on the reading of a single chapter.

When you read only a sliver of a book, you may be able to surmise a bit of information about a character's personality, catch a glimpse of the setting, or experience some measure of triumph or defeat. However, without an understanding of the overarching narrative of the novel, your analysis of a single chapter will be obscured and shallow at best. You would be left wondering...

What are the character's motivations? Why do the events in this small snippet of story matter? Why should I care about what's happening? A teacher would never invent such a ridiculous assignment because all true scholars know that the ultimate meaning of any passage is lost without context.

This may seem like a silly example, yet this is how many of us have been trained to read the Bible. We see the Word as an anthology of stand-alone stories or lists of principles to follow. When we read a passage of Scripture without understanding its place in the Bible's larger story, we miss its true meaning and application.

As Eugene Peterson says, "It takes the whole Bible to read any part of the Bible."[1]

The Bible is really one cohesive, magnificent story that reveals God's character and His intentions for us. Sally Lloyd Jones explains, "There are lots of stories in the Bible, but all the stories are telling one Big Story. The Story of how God loves His children and came to rescue them. It takes the whole Bible to tell this story...Every story in the Bible whispers His name."[2] Though Scripture does tell mankind who we really are and why we're here, humans are not its primary characters. The Bible is a story written by God and about God.

Biblical culturalist Kristi McLelland points out that our western approach to Scripture has been heavily influenced by Greco-Roman thought. This causes us to go to the text and ask the question, "What does this have to do with me?" In the East, readers approach the text with an entirely different question, "What does this have to teach me about God?"[3]

This distinction can be noted in the way they refer to the parables of Christ. I grew up hearing stories called, "The Prodigal Son," and, "The Lost Sheep." In the East, they grow up hearing stories about, "The Running Father," and, "The Good Shepherd."[4]

We Westerners want desperately to find ourselves in the text. Ironically, this approach does nothing but muddy the waters of accurate self-perception, because "We can't know who we are until we know who God is."(5)

Each word of the Bible was "God-breathed" (2 Timothy 3:16, NIV) and carefully selected to reveal a piece of Himself to us, His beloved. If we miss Him, we miss everything. When we lean in close to the text with intention and expectation, we will hear His heartbeat thrumming through each carefully, curated word.

> *"The genius of the biblical story is what it tells us about God Himself; A God who sacrifices Himself in death out of love for His enemies; a God who would rather experience the death we deserved than to be apart from the people He created for His pleasure...A God who would not let us go, but who would pursue us — all of us, even the worst of us — so that He might restore us into joyful fellowship with Himself."(6)*

So what is this bigger story?

This overarching storyline is referred to as the "metanarrative" of Scripture and is broken down into four parts.

Creation

GOD CREATED THE WORLD AND EVERYTHING IN IT, PROCLAIMING IT "GOOD" (GENESIS 1:31). HUMANS WERE SET APART AS THE "CROWNING GLORY OF THE CREATOR'S WORK — BEINGS MADE IN GOD'S OWN LIKENESS, WITH WHOM HE COULD COMMUNE, AND IN WHOM HE COULD DELIGHT, BEINGS WHO WOULD KNOW THE SHEER PLEASURE OF HIS PRESENCE, LOVE, AND FAVOR." (7) THE FIRST HUMANS LIVED IN PERFECT FELLOWSHIP WITH GOD AND WITH EACH OTHER IN A GARDEN OF PERFECT BEAUTY AND PERFECT PEACE.

Fall

HUMANS CHOSE TO REBEL AGAINST GOD, SEVERING THEIR RELATIONSHIP WITH HIM AND WITH EACH OTHER. HUMANS NOW LIVE AS SLAVES TO DISTORTED, SINFUL PASSIONS WHICH WILL NEVER SATISFY. OUR GREATEST EFFORTS TO OBTAIN RIGHTEOUSNESS AND FAVOR WITH GOD FALL SHORT. WE ARE LIKE, "SHEEP" WHO HAVE "GONE ASTRAY," (ISAIAH 53:6) AND ARE DESERVING OF BOTH PHYSICAL AND ETERNAL DEATH, TRAGICALLY SEPARATED FROM OUR CREATOR.

Redemption —

Though our sins have condemned us as worthy of death, God still loved us. "For God so loved the world, that he gave his only Son, that whoever believes in him should not perish but have eternal life" (John 3:16). In his great mercy, the Father enacted the greatest rescue plan of all time — he sent Christ to earth to live a sinless life and to die as a sacrificial atonement for our sins. Humans cannot earn their way back to God, but when we place our faith in Christ and in what he accomplished for us on the cross, we can be forgiven and made new. "By his crucifixion and resurrection [he] made possible our being restored to the image of God...and through the gift of the Spirit became present with us in constant fellowship."(8)

Restoration

This final chapter of the story hasn't been lived out yet. One day Christ will return to take his rightful place as King of the universe. He will create a new heaven, and a new earth, abolishing death and pain and sin forever. Humans will enjoy perfect fellowship with God and with each other for all eternity.

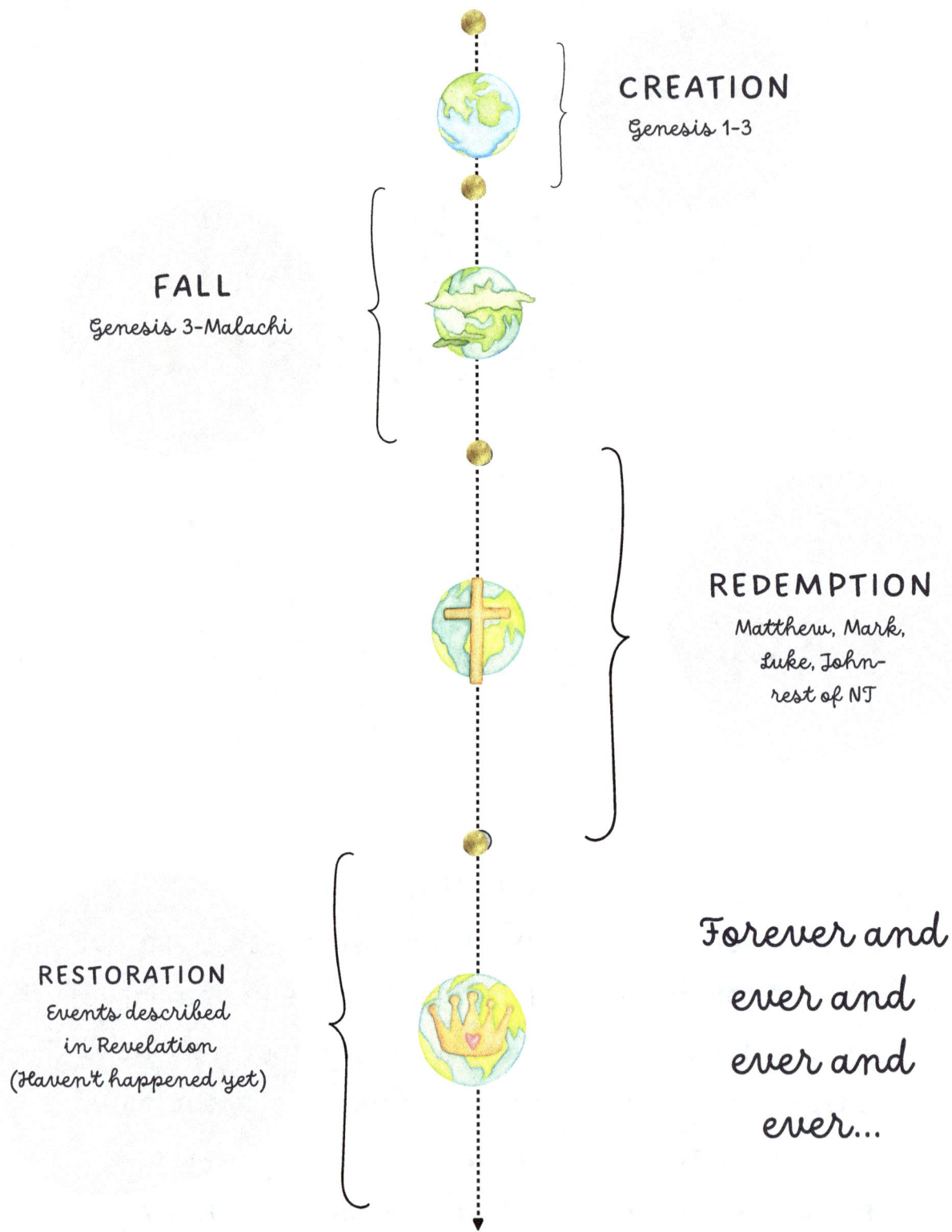

The restoration is the ultimate happily ever after. I love how Trilia Newbell summarizes this incredible tale ... "GOD MADE IT. PEOPLE RUINED IT. HE RESCUED IT. HE WILL FINISH it."(9)

If we were to sort the Bible chronologically according to these themes, Genesis 1-2 would speak of creation, Genesis 3 would describe the fall, while the rest of the Old Testament would be spent detailing the ramifications of this tragedy and the hope of a coming Savior. Beginning in Matthew, God's plan for redemption is fully revealed in the life of Christ. We witness the power of Christ's resurrection to transform fallen humanity throughout the rest of the New Testament. The book of Revelation describes the events that will take place during the restoration.

This does not mean that the discussion of these themes is limited to their earthly time frame. One of the breathtakingly beautiful aspects of the Bible is its seamless stitching of the Gospel story throughout all of its 66 books.

In Israel, they refer to individual Bible stories as "pearls." As Mclelland says, "Each story is like a pearl, beautiful and of great price on its own. But what's more beautiful is stringing the biblical pearls together."(10)

When we're looking for them, we can find "pearls" of redemption which wind their way from the Garden to the empty grave. We find God covering shame in Eden, the sacrifice of a firstborn son in Abraham and Isaac, the protective covering of the blood of a slain lamb in Egypt, and a vivid description of the horrors of the crucifixion in Isaiah, written hundreds of years before Jesus came to earth.

We will miss the significance of these passages if we don't see them as pieces in the Bible's cohesive "strand" of story. I want our hearts to be trained to look at the Word and see a beautiful "necklace" of truth rather than a series of disjointed poems and parables.
I don't think it's a coincidence that Jesus refers to life in the Kingdom of God, to the life found in Him, as "The Pearl of Greatest Price,"(Matthew 13:45-46) in the gospels. When we understand that every piece of the Word is designed to reveal the heart of Christ to us, even the most frequently ignored passages of Scriptures come alive with meaning. It will take some effort to mine these jewels from the rich soil of the Word.
As John Piper says, "The Bible will not give its riches to those who will not dig."(11)
So let's pull on some gloves and unpack our shovels. There's treasure to be found!

How precious is your steadfast love, O God! The children of mankind take refuge in the shadow of your wings Psalm 36:7 And I will betroth you to me forever. I will betroth you to me in righteousness and in justice, in steadfast love and in mercy Hosea 2:19 The steadfast love of the Lord never ceases; his mercies never come to an end; they are new every morning; great is your faithfulness Lamentations 3:22-23 "I have loved you with an everlasting love; therefore I have continued my faithfulness to you. Jeremiah 31:3 How precious is your steadfast love, O God! The children of mankind take refuge in the shadow of your wings Psalm 36:7 And I will betroth you to me forever. I will betroth you to me in righteousness and in justice, in steadfast love and in mercy Hosea 2:19 The steadfast love of the Lord never ceases; his mercies never come to an end; they are new every morning; great is your faithfulness Lamentations 3:22-23 "I have loved you with an everlasting love; therefore I have continued my faithfulness to you. Jeremiah 31:3 How precious is your steadfast love, O God! The children of mankind take refuge in the shadow of your wings Psalm 36:7 And I will betroth you to me forever. I will betroth you to me in righteousness and in justice, in steadfast love and in mercy Hosea 2:19 The steadfast love of the Lord never ceases; his mercies never come to an end; they are new every morning; great is your faithfulness Lamentations 3:22-23 "I have loved you with an everlasting love; therefore I have continued my faithfulness to you. Jeremiah 31:3 How precious is your steadfast love, O God! The children of mankind take refuge in the shadow of your wings Psalm 36:7 And I will betroth you to me forever. I will betroth you to me in righteousness and in justice, in steadfast love and in mercy Hosea 2:19 The steadfast love of the Lord never ceases; his mercies never come to an end; they are new every morning; great is your faithfulness Lamentations 3:22-23 "I have loved you with an everlasting love; therefore I have continued my faithfulness to you. Jeremiah 31:3 How pre

WHAT'S MORE BEAUTIFUL
THAN A SINGLE PEARL IS
A STRING OF PEARLS.

-Kristi Mclelland

Invitation To Intimacy

The more we soak ourselves in the grander story of Scripture, the more we will see the Bible as less of a textbook and more of a romance.

How many movies have you seen, books have you read, where the storyline focuses on a lovestruck man who risks all to woo and to rescue a woman? There is a reason we are mesmerized by tales of a man who will give anything to get the girl.

Every great love story on earth is patterned after the plotline of the cross.

Yet, the cross is no fairytale, and the real Hero of History has His eyes set on *you*. Our God *did* give everything to get the girl. When we see Scripture as a cohesive whole, we won't find a Christ who demands holiness from His followers like a Heavenly Headmaster hovering over us with a yardstick. We find a God who pursues us like a lovesick Groom who would do anything to remove what stands in the way of union with His beloved.

One of my favorite "strand of pearls" in the Bible is the symbolism of marriage. Did you know the Bible begins and ends with a wedding? In Genesis 3, we find the God-ordained union of Adam and Eve. In Revelation 21, we find the celebration of the centuries, the party to end all parties — the Wedding Feast of the Lamb. Where our Christ is crowned King forever and we, His people, are finally and forever united to our Beloved. (You should go check it out for yourself!)

Though the first recorded marriage in the Bible is between a human man and woman, Paul makes it clear in Ephesians 5:25-32, that human marriage is somehow patterned *after* Christ's relationship with His Church.

> *Husbands, love your wives, as Christ loved the church and gave Himself up for her, that He might sanctify her, having cleansed her by the washing of the water with the Word, so that He might present the church to Himself in splendor, without spot or wrinkle or any such thing, that might be holy and without blemish. In the same way, husbands should love their wives as their own bodies, He who loves His wife loves himself. For no one ever hated his own flesh, but nourishes and cherishes it, just as Christ does the church, because we are members of His body. 'Therefore a man shall leave his father and mother hold fast to his wife, and the two shall become one flesh.' This mystery is profound, and I am saying that it refers to Christ and the church.*

Obviously, Paul is not speaking of marriage in the physical, sensual human understanding of the word. He's talking about a union of *souls rather than a union of skin.*
Sinclair Ferguson describes union with Christ in this way,

"Through the work of the Spirit, the heavenly Father gives you to Jesus and gives Jesus to you. You have Him. Everything you can ever lack is found in Him; all you ever need is given to you in Him... For the Father has "blessed us in Christ with every spiritual blessing in the heavenly places."(1)

He doesn't take our sin away to be nit-picky or to take away our fun. Christ faced down death and paid with His own blood to wipe us clean of everything that separated us from Him.

He makes us like Jesus, so we can *have Jesus*. "This is the gospel — not any benefit Christ brings, but that, above all, Christ brings us into communion with God."(2)

When we receive Christ, we immediately become, "new creatures," (2 Corinthians 5:17) and are forever forgiven in God's sight. However, this does not mean our outward behavior immediately aligns with our new identity as a child of God. This entire earth journey is a process of our gradual conformity to the Image of Christ. Our divine metamorphosis, called "sanctification," will not be complete until the day we see our Savior Face to face.

"Beloved, we are God's children now, and what we will be has not yet appeared; but we know that when he appears we shall be like him, because we shall see him as he is. Everyone who has this hope purifies himself even as he is pure"(1 John 3:2).

We don't become like Jesus because we *have to*; we become like Jesus because we *want to*, because we have determined that Jesus is the One our soul loves, and we want all of Him that we can get. Christ wants us to be so secure in His affections, so enthralled with our Groom and our future with Him, that we delight in the process of spiritual growth like a bride delights in planning for her wedding day.

Is there any creature on earth so alive, so radiant, as an engaged woman?

We gleefully pore over table settings and color schemes, create four Pinterest boards full of floral arrangements and clever, hand-made favors. And the dress, oh, the dress. We spend our lives dreaming and sketching and imagining our groom's reaction to seeing us in our gown of glory! This euphoric level of "blushing bride" excitement is what Christ had in mind for us when He chose the cross. We should be as excited, as meticulous, as dedicated to preparing our hearts to meet our Heavenly Bridegroom, as we are in preparing ourselves for our earthly wedding day.

for the fine linen is the righteous deeds of the saints. And the angel said [a] Blessed are those who are invited to the marriage supper of the Lamb." And are the true words of God." Then I fell down at his feet to worship him, but must not do that! I am a fellow servant with you and your brothers who hold us. Worship God." For the testimony of Jesus is the spirit of prophecy. ed are those who wash their robes, so that they may have the right to the tre y enter the city by the gates. Outside are the dogs and sorcerers and the sexu rderers and idolaters, and everyone who loves and practices falsehood. "I, Jes et to testify to you about these things for the churches. I am the root and the de , the bright morning star." The Spirit and the Bride say, "Come." And let say, "Come." And let the one who is thirsty come; let the one who desires tak out price. I warn everyone who ___ ords of the prophecy of this book God will add to him the plagues ___ in this book, 19 and if anyone takes of the book of this prophecy, God ___ way his share in the tree of life hich are described in this boo ___ to these things says, "Sure Amen. Come, Lord Jes ___ Jesus be with all. Ame Let us rejoice and exu ___ marriage of the Lamb ride has made herself ___ herself with fine line for the fine linen is ___ d the angel said [a] Blessed are those w ___ he Lamb." And are the true wor ___ rship him, but must not do that! ___ rs who hold us. Worship ___ prophecy. ed are those ___ to the tre

For our earthly husbands, we start new workout routines and head to the tanning bed. For our forever Love, we, through His Spirit working in us, ditch old habits and learn how to live in sacrificial love.

When we see our destiny as the Wedding Feast of the Lamb, where we are not just a name on the guest list, but the one wearing white and walking the aisle, our view on the Bible changes.

> ***The call to seek Christ in Scripture should feel less like an assignment and more like an invitation to intimacy.***

Listen to how the apostle Peter described what he believed should be the normative Christian experience. "Though you have not seen him, you love him. Though you do not now see him, you believe in him and rejoice with joy that is inexpressible and filled with glory"(1 Peter 1:8).

Have you ever wondered why some Christians seem to have a close relationship with God, experiencing this supernatural joy, while others are dragging through life as if He's not even there?

Although Christ has promised never to leave us or forsake us, and has joined us to Himself in permanent, unbreakable union despite our continued sin, our practical experience of Him can be quite different depending on our response to His invitation. A married couple with a strained relationship can live in the same house, yet feel a million miles away from one another. Their union as husband and wife is still intact, but their communion with each other is lacking. In the same way, theologian John Owen points out that there is a crucial difference between *union* with God and *communion* with God.

"Those who are united to Christ are called to respond to God's loving embrace. While union with Christ is something that does not ebb and flow, one's experience of communion with Christ can fluctuate."(3)

Sister, there is no divine divorce in your future. He is faithful even when we are not. Unfortunately, many of us choose not to experience the benefits of union with Christ and spend our lives chasing lesser treasures. Spurgeon reminds us, "There is no joy in this world like union with Christ. The more we can feel it, the happier we are."(4)

So, how do we live in such a way that we can feel the full weight of His love? How do we stoke the fires of divine intimacy?

I want to introduce three practical ways our communion with Christ is enhanced.

John 4:24 God is spirit, and those who worship him must worship in spirit and truth. John 4:24 God is spirit, and those who worship him must worship in spirit and truth. John 4:24 God is spirit, and those who worship him must worship in spirit and truth. John 4:24 God is spirit, and those who worship him must worship in spirit and truth. John 4:24 God is spirit, and those who worship him must worship in spirit and truth. John 4:24 God is spirit, and those who worship him must worship in spirit and truth. John 4:24 God is spirit, and those who worship him must worship in spirit and truth. John 4:24 God is spirit, and those who worship him must worship in spirit and truth. John 4:24 God is spirit, and those who worship him must worship in spirit and truth. John 4:24 God is spirit, and those who worship him must worship in spirit and truth. John 4:24 God is spirit, and those who worship him must worship in spirit and truth. John 4:24 God is spirit, and those who worship him must worship in spirit and truth. John 4:24 God is spirit, and those who worship him must worship in spirit and truth. John 4:24 God is spirit, and those who worship him must worship in spirit and truth. John 4:24 God is spirit, and those who worship him must worship in spirit and truth. John 4:24 God is spirit, and those who worship him must worship in spirit and truth. John 4:24 God is spirit, and those who worship him must worship in spirit and truth. John 4:24 God is spirit, and those who worship him must worship in spirit and truth. John 4:24 God is spirit, and those who worship him must worship in spirit and truth. John 4:24 God is spirit, and those who worship him must worship in spirit and truth. John 4:24 God is spirit, and those who worship him must worship in spirit and truth. John 4:24 God is spirit, and those who worship him must worship in spirit and truth.

MAYBE WE THINK OF GOD AND CHRIST IN TERMS OF TRUTH, NOT BEAUTY. BUT THE WHOLE REASON WE CARE ABOUT SOUND DOCTRINE IS FOR THE SAKE OF PRESERVING GOD'S BEAUTY, JUST AS THE WHOLE REASON WE CARE ABOUT EFFECTIVE FOCAL LENSES ON A CAMERA IS TO CAPTURE WITH PRECISION THE BEAUTY WE PHOTOGRAPH.

-Dane Ortlund

Intimacy Begins With Information

Hang around church long enough and you're sure to hear the phrase, "head knowledge versus heart knowledge." The concept is simple -- God is not interested in our ability to rattle off a series of facts about Him. As we just discussed, He is interested in a personal, experiential, love relationship with us.

God demonstrates this in His Word from beginning to end that He has more in mind for us than outward conformity to a set of standards or traditions. When the nation of Israel attempted to cover up their continual idolatry with ritualistic sacrifices, God cried, "I want you to show love, not offer sacrifices. I want you to know Me more than I want burnt offerings" (Hosea 6:6 NLT). The religious leaders of Christ's day practiced strict adherence to the Mosaic Law and had likely memorized huge chunks of the Old Testament. (It hurt my brain to memorize the names of the books of the Old Testament. I can't imagine trying to cram a large bulk of their contents into my mind. These guys were like the Bible quizzing champions of the ancient world. They *kept* all the rules, they *knew* it all.

You'd think Jesus would be handing them medals, pointing them out as great examples to follow. Instead, Jesus called them, "Whitewashed tombs, which look beautiful on the outside but on the inside are full of the bones of the dead and everything unclean" (Matthew 23:27-28, NIV). Again and again He chastised them, explaining, "This people honors Me with their lips, but their heart is far from Me" (Matthew 15:8).

What words could be more chilling coming from the mouth of the Son of God? I think we can all bring a few modern-day Pharisees to mind: the lead Sunday school teacher who is also the town gossip, the elder who mistreats his wife, the pastor's kid who parties every Saturday night. My concern is that in a valiant effort to distance ourselves from these harmful, cultural stereotypes, we sometimes swing too far in the opposite direction, and try to skip the head and go straight for the heart.

We ditch the heavy doctrine for more emotionally stimulating subjects. We limit talk about the rules because after all, "Christianity is not a religion, it's a relationship." While I wholeheartedly agree with this statement, we must remember, "The heart cannot love what the mind does not know."(1)

We can know *about* God without loving Him. But we cannot love Him in the way He desires without accurate, ever-deepening knowledge of Him.

In Christ's famous encounter with the woman at the well, He said that the Father is seeking true worshipers who will, "worship the Father in spirit and in truth" (John 4:24).

In other words, ***head knowledge is not the enemy of heart knowledge***.

This is not an either/or situation. We need both solid doctrine and spirited passion to worship and experience Jesus in the white-hot way He desires. We cannot have true love, without well, *truth*.

When we look at Scripture carefully, we can see that the trajectory of real love for God does not go from heart to head, but from head to heart. In Romans 12:1-2, Paul says, "Do not be conformed to this world, but be transformed by the renewal of your mind, that by testing you may discern what is the will of God, what is good and acceptable and perfect."

Wilkin explains,

> *As we grow in the knowledge of God's character through the study of His Word, we cannot help but grow into an exponentially deeper love for Him. This explains why Romans 12:2 says we are transformed by the renewing of our minds. We come to understand who God is, and we are changed — our affections detach from lesser things and attach to Him.(2)*

There is great value in listening to others teach about Jesus, but the Word of God is the ONE place we can go and know with 100% certainty that we will find accurate information about the Almighty. On the night Jesus was arrested, He prayed for His disciples, begging the Father to, "Sanctify them by Your truth, Your Word is truth" (John 17:17).

Now the question becomes, "How do I get knowledge to move from my head to heart?"

I GIVE MY LIFE

TO SPEND AND BE SPENT FOR YOU

I GIVE MY SONG

TO BE TOUCHED BY YOUR FIRE AND CONSUMED

SOME SAY IT'S WASTEFUL

BUT THEY DON'T KNOW YOU

I GIVE MY LOVE

AND I GET YOU

—Laura Hackett

Intimacy Requires Intentionality

Sometimes, my sweet husband, Kyle, will write, "I love you," on little slips of paper and hide them all around the house for me to find. He has put them in the bread box, in the refrigerator, and in the pocket of his pants where he knew I'd check before throwing them in the washer.

I feel like I am on a constant treasure hunt to find these tiny, tangible proofs of my husband's love. I don't seek out and read these notes in the same way I would complete a homework assignment. I cherish each little scrap of paper, and fawn over his familiar, handwritten script, because they came from the heart of a real-life person who wants to express his real-life love to me.

In the same way, we shouldn't approach the Bible like we approach a textbook written by a stranger. We need to approach the Word as if a personal God is waiting there to meet with us.

"Seek the words of Jesus as living words — words that come not in the abstract but come from the heart and on the lips of a living Person whom we love more than any other Person in the world."(1)

The way we relate to the Bible is vastly different from the way we relate to any other text. The Bible is the only book in the world where the Author is not only still living, but is living inside of us in the form of the Holy Spirit.

"We never just read the Bible, we interact with it. It is living and active and so are we. In the mouth of the Jews, they would say that anytime we touch the sacred Scriptures, it is life with life."(2)

My husband and I had a long-distance, dating relationship. During that time, nothing thrilled my heart so much as a text or call from Kyle. I couldn't see him in person, so every emoji, every piece of information, every hint of affection I could gather from him, was precious. The highlight of my day was the glorious hour before bed when I could shut my door and share a goodnight "Facetime" call, soaking up every word, and enjoying every detail of the man I was soon to marry.

I didn't learn things about Kyle because he was going to quiz me at the end of the night about his likes and dislikes. I wanted to learn things about Kyle because he was (and still is) the most fascinating human in my world and it is my greatest joy to know him more. My study of Kyle is personal. I want to know him more because I want my relationship with him to deepen.

Do we approach our times with the Lord like I approached my nightly call with Kyle? Does our heart thrill and yearn to be alone with Him? Do we yearn to know Him more so that we can love Him more?

When we see our personal Bible study as our time to meet with our Forever Bridegroom, our attitude changes.

Our time in the Word should feel less like a chore and more like falling in love.

Now that we've seen how we should come to the Word, let's talk about how often.

My husband and grandfather are currently obsessed with the reality TV show, *Alone*. At the beginning of each season, 10 contestants are dropped off in the middle of an untamed wilderness and forced to survive on their own. The last one to "tap out" wins! (This setup is literally my worst nightmare. I will take my electricity, heated blanket, and bubble bath, thank you very much!)

As a result of my family's current infatuation, I have watched a lot of people building fires from scratch. The people on this show have to constantly keep a fire going or they will simultaneously freeze and starve.

Fire is literally *life* to these stranded survivalists.

One thing I've noticed about these fires is that they never seem to start themselves. The contestants have to do something to cause the wood to ignite, whether it's to strike a flint or create a friction fire. For a spark to happen, there must be contact.

No one ever gathers their supplies, makes a nice little pile of wood chips, and then sits back and stares at the pile of debris, waiting for it to ignite. No one makes a fire pit in their backyard, invites a bunch of people over, and then just sits there holding a bag of marshmallows, expecting the bonfire to light on command.

Fire doesn't work this way. You have to CREATE the spark if you want a flame.

In the same way, you have to make CONTACT with the Word of God in order for your heart to catch on fire. The mere presence of a Bible in your house or on your nightstand is not going to fan your affection for God into flame. You have to open it and put your heart on His heart like a flint to a stone if you want spiritual sparks to fly.

Another thing I've noticed about fires is that if you forget to feed them, they will burn out. I have personal experience with this process since we usually supplement the heat in our West Virginia farmhouse with a wood stove. During the harsh, winter months, my grandfather faithfully rises morning and night to squeak open the stove's coal-black doors and shove a log into the spitting, orange embers. Once we get the fire started, he is usually able to keep the same fire going for the entire winter without having to restart it a single time.

I remember one particular occasion when I awoke to a cold, dark living room, and knew instantly that the fire had gone out. The difference was palpable and uncomfortable.

Have you woken up to a cold heart instead of a cold house?

Your relationship with Christ will lack sparks if you're not making contact with Him. If we only brush shoulders with Christ on Sunday and aren't feeding our souls throughout the week, then we'll spend our days like a pile of smoking embers instead of the walking wildfires He envisioned.

...he takes away, and every branch that does bear fruit he prunes, that it may bear more... ready you are clean because of the word that I have spoken to you. 4 Abide in me, and... the branch cannot bear fruit by itself, unless it abides in the vine, neither can you, unless... in me. 5 I am the vine; you are the branches. Whoever abides in me and I in him... bears much fruit, for apart from me you can do nothing. 6 If anyone does not abide in... own away like a branch and withers; and the branches are gathered, thrown into the fire... ed. 7 If you abide in me, and my words abide in you, ask whatever you wish, and it... ou. 8 By this my Father is glorified, that you bear much fruit and so prove to be m... s the Father has loved me, so have I loved you. Abide in my love. " If you keep m... andments, you will abide in my love, just as I have kept my Father's commandments... s love. 11 These things I have spoken to you, that my joy may be in you, and that you... ll." This is my commandment, that you love one another as I have loved you. 13 Great... no one than this, that someone lay down his life for his friends. 14 You are my friend... I command you. 15 No longer do I call you servants,[a] for the servant does not kn... master is doing; but I have called you friends, for all that I have heard from my Fa... made known to you. 16 You did not choose me, but I chose you and appointed you that... d bear fruit and that your fruit should abide, so that whatever you ask the Father in... ay give it to you. 17 These things I command you, so that you will love one another... the true vine, and my Father is the vinedresser. 2 Every branch in me that does n... he takes away, and every branch that does bear fruit he prunes, that it may bear more... ready you are clean because of the word that I have spoken to you. 4 Abide in me, an... the branch cannot bear fruit by itself, unless it abides in the vine, neither can you, unl... in me. 5 I am the vine; you are the branches. Whoever abides in me and I in him... bears much fruit, for apart from me you can do nothing. 6 If anyone does not abide in... own away like a branch and withers; and the branches are gathered, thrown into the fir... ed. 7 If you abide in me, and my words abide in you, ask whatever you wish, and it... ou. 8 By this my Father is glorified, that you bear much fruit and so prove to be m...

I'M RETURNING TO THE SECRET PLACE

JUST AN ALTAR AND A FLAME

LOVE IS FOUND HERE IN OUR SACRED SPACE

I HEAR YOUR VOICE, I SEE YOUR FACE

-Kari Jobe

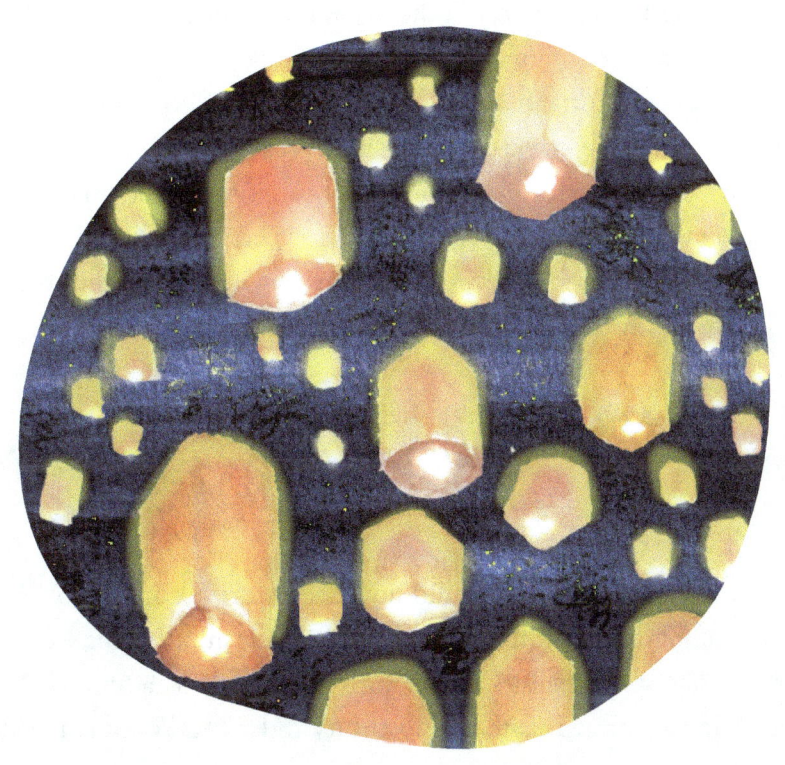

Intimacy Is Ignited Through Obedience

When I was in college, I hung a sticky note on my study cubicle that read, "To live to know Him means that I must die and Christ must live through me."

I am not sure where this quote originated, however, I do remember that when I first tacked it up on my wall, I didn't fully grasp its meaning. I put it right where I could see it because I desperately wanted to understand its message.

My heart's greatest desire was to know Jesus more, but it seemed to me that this self-denying obedience was more of an Old Testament thing. Didn't Christ die so that I wouldn't have to worry so much about obedience and could just enjoy Him?

I was right in some aspects.

Christ redeemed us so that we could enjoy the full blessing of restored fellowship with Him.

Obedience *doesn't* earn our salvation.

What I failed to understand was crucial.

When we are in Christ, obedience ceases to become a burden and becomes our means of enjoying Jesus. As Chip Ingram says, "Obedience is the organ through which intimacy with God is obtained."(1)

Jesus lays out the end result of obedience in John 15:10, "If you keep my commandments, you will abide in my love, just as I have kept my Father's commandments and abide in His love. These things I have spoken to you, that My joy may be in you and that your joy may be full."

This passage caused me some initial hesitation. It seemed that Christ was saying we had to obey Him in order to earn His love. We know this is not true because He assures us over and over throughout Scripture that His love for us will never fail and is not based on our performance. "To be clear, the love of God for us does not change, but our experience of his love does."(2)

When I began to grasp the difference between union with God and communion with God, this verse and the sticky note on my wall took on a whole new meaning.

Obedience is not a harsh, life-draining obligation, it is an invitation to joy.

In the last portion, we discussed how God did not save us so we could know Him in a textbook sense, but so we could know Him in an intimate, love relationship. In this section, we will discuss how the gift of the Holy Spirit enables us to do more than just admire His heart from afar. Through obedience, He has offered us the opportunity to let His Word come alive in us and for His heart to beat through our own.

My favorite passage of scripture is found in Philippians 3, where Paul discusses how his desire to know Christ has consumed him,

> *Indeed, I count everything as loss because of the surpassing worth of knowing Christ Jesus my Lord. For His sake I have suffered the loss of all things and count them as rubbish, in order that I may gain Christ and be found in Him...that I may know Him and the power of His resurrection, and may share His sufferings, becoming like Him in His death, that by any means possible I may attain the resurrection from the dead (Philippians 3:8-10).*

The "knowing" Paul is speaking of here is not academic, it is experiential. Paul wants to stay so surrendered and in such touch with the Spirit that his everyday choices become a living exploration of Christ.

Paul's not just reading about Jesus.

Paul's literally living out Jesus.

"For I am crucified with Christ, and yet I live. Yet not I but Christ who lives within me" (Galatians 2:20).

Like Paul, all true believers have been "crucified" with Christ.

"There is a union between Christ and Christians so that what happened to Christ is counted by God as happening to us. His death is our death."(3) We get to skip the punishment we deserve and are credited the righteousness only Christ deserves.

However, unlike Paul, not every believer experiences Jesus living through them on a daily basis. Paul understood that being "crucified with Christ" does not exempt the believer from Jesus' call to, "take up your cross daily and follow Me" (Luke 9:23).

When Christ chose the cross, He established the pattern for our entrance into true life.

His death became the gateway to our eternal resurrection.

Our daily choice to die to self becomes the gateway to experiencing eternal life here and now.

Eternal life doesn't begin when we get to Heaven. As Tony Evans says, "The resurrection is not an event. The resurrection is a Person."(4) Knowing and living in relationship with the One who conquered death *is* life, now and forever.

Jesus said, "This is eternal life, that they may know You, the one True God, and Jesus Christ, whom You have sent" (John 17:3).

We say, "yes," to this incredible invitation when we choose to deny the flesh and let Christ live through us. In some crazy way, obedience not only becomes our way of loving God, it becomes our way of letting Him love us.

When we are in Christ, choosing to obey is like opening a present. We have a good Father who is not going to settle for giving us lesser things.

He wants to give us Himself.

He wants to trade our anxiety for His peace, the stain of lust for His purity, the incessant need for more for the quiet waters of contentment, the ugly grip of bitterness for restored relationships.

When we choose to disobey, we are essentially telling God that we think we can take better care of ourselves than He can. We are saying we don't trust Him to fulfill our desires.

When we see what God says in His Word, and we make the choice to put it into action, no matter how difficult the task, we are speaking God's love language.

Obedience is saying, "I trust You, Lord. You hold my best interest at heart. I'm gonna let You take care of me YOUR way. I'm declaring to the world that You are worth it and worthy of my obedience!"

I'm gonna let You love me.

And He responds, "Oh, darling, I've just been waiting to hear you say that. Get ready for a white-knuckle ride of an adventure!"

Our God never intended for the Bible to remain motionless words on a page.

The Bible is not just a book to be read, but an adventure to be lived.

This epic journey winds its way through the ordinary stuff of life — when we choose to serve a hungry child rather than feed ourselves. When we forgive our co-workers one more time. When we choose to do that annoying task without complaint.

The kitchen, the car, the work cubicle: these are the sacred spaces where intimacy happens. I bought a sign that reads, "*This must be the place*," and positioned it above my kitchen sink to help me remember that surrender can make any place a holy place. A crusty casserole dish can become a collision with the divine.

Obedience transforms our routine into a romance.

We live out the amazing truth that, "God is most glorified in us when we are most satisfied in Him."(5)

"Union with Christ is an enchanted reality. It tells us that the most important things about our lives cannot be seen or touched with our senses. It tells us that there are extraordinary depths running just below the surface of our lives."(6)

As I searched for a way to succinctly summarize these ideas, God dropped the answer right into my lap, more like into my pastor's mind.

This past week's sermon was a perfect summary of God's roadmap toward the abundant life.(6)

Basic principles of psychology dictate the pattern for human behavior modification:

WE CHANGE THE WAY WE …
Think

WHICH CHANGES THE WAY WE…
Act

WHICH CHANGES THE WAY WE …
Feel

We get in ginormous trouble when we let our feelings drive our actions. If we wait to act until we get just the right emotion, we might never do the right thing. Proper emotions are the reward for acting the right way.

Isn't it amazing how the Bible said it first?

WE CHANGE THE WAY WE ...
Think

REAL HEART CHANGE HAPPENS WHEN WE CHANGE OUR MINDS.

WHICH CHANGES THE WAY WE...
Act

REAL HEART CHANGE HAPPENS WHEN WE APPROACH HIM WITH INTENTIONALITY AND FOLLOW THROUGH WITH OBEDIENCE.

WHICH CHANGES THE WAY WE ...
Feel

REAL JOY COMES AFTER WE ACT. THE JOY JESUS PROMISES HAPPENS ON THE OTHER SIDE OF SURRENDER.

This is not hypocrisy or behaving like a Pharisee. "This is acting in faith." Have your emotions for Christ cooled? Don't be afraid. "There is no such thing as a dead relationship."(8)

God gives us the plan for re-igniting the fire in Revelation 2, where He addresses the believers at the ancient church in Ephesus. These believers had remained faithful under persecution and not compromised on doctrine, however, they had lost their initial passion for God.

> *"But I have this against you, that you have abandoned the love you had at first. Remember therefore from where you have fallen; repent, and do the works you did at first."*
> *(Revelation 2:4-5)*

WE CHANGE THE WAY WE …

THINK

WE REMEMBER,
AND WE REPENT (CHANGE OUR MINDS)

WHICH CHANGES THE WAY WE…

ACT

WE DO THE THINGS WE DID
AT FIRST.

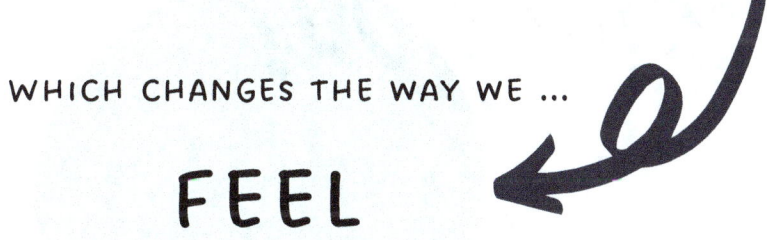

WHICH CHANGES THE WAY WE …

FEEL

GOD REAWAKENS A SLEEPING
PASSION.

I don't normally experience spiritual epiphanies while watching television, however I was recently deeply touched by a scene from the show, *Manifest*. In this series, a group of passengers takes a flight home one evening only to discover their plane has landed five years in the future. One of the main characters, Ben, discovers his wife's love for him has faded during his time away. In desperation, he tells her, "I know your love for me is out of practice, like a memory...for me, it was only yesterday. I never forgot. So please, for us, remember. *Remember.*"(9)

Unlike us, God's passion for His beloved has never wavered or dimmed, even for a moment. Even if we have forgotten what it's like to love Him, *He remembers.*

For Him, it was always just, "Yesterday."

You are not just a flash in God's memory. He is in your present, holding out His hand, knocking on your heart's door, ready to come in and dine with you.

Will you let Him love you?

YOU'RE STILL MY FIRST LOVE
YOU'RE STILL MY ONLY ONE
THERE'S A TABLE JUST FOR YOU AND ME
BREAK THE BREAD AND POUR THE WINE
PERFECT UNION, NOTHING IN BETWEEN
I AM YOURS AND YOU ARE MINE
I FEEL MY HEART BEATING OUT OF MY CHEST
I WANNA STAY FOREVER LIKE THIS
MAY THE FLAME OF MY HEART ALWAYS BE LIT
I WANNA BURN FOREVER LIKE THIS

-Kari Jobe

Turn my eyes from looking at worthless things; and give me life in your ways. Psalm 119:37 I have made a covenant with my eyes Job 31:1 Keep your heart with all vigilance, for from it flow the springs of life. Proverbs 4:23

"WE DESTROY ARGUMENTS AND EVERY LOFTY OPINION
RAISED AGAINST THE KNOWLEDGE OF GOD,
AND TAKE EVERY THOUGHT CAPTIVE TO OBEY CHRIST."

2 Corinthians 2:5

Romancing The Mind

I didn't want to write this chapter.

I knew that in the process of researching this information, I would be forced to examine my own habits and make some real, possibly painful, changes.

For a long time, I have perused articles about social media addiction and the dangers of smartphone dependence and excused myself from their warnings.

"This doesn't apply to me," I would say, "I'm not looking at filth. I'm looking at newborn babies and new paint colors for my kitchen. I'm not one of those distracted moms that sits around on her phone all day. I'm engaged! I play with my kids. I can't give up Facebook, I use it for ministry."

On the surface level, my phone usage was mild. What I had been refusing to see was the internal havoc my phone was wreaking on my mind and on my soul, and most importantly, *my relationship with Christ*.

For the Christian, the danger of the digital world lies in far more than the quality of the content we choose to intake. We must be just as vigilant about the *manner* in which we consume media.

"How we consume is as important as what we consume."[1]

For most of us, the way we are using our phones is changing the way we think and the way we feel satisfied. That's a big deal because, "If the way we're using entertainment erodes our ability to reflect, reason, and savor truth, it erodes our ability to know and enjoy Jesus."[2]

Do you find yourself reaching for your phone compulsively every few minutes?

Do you feel uneasy when you go a long stretch without checking your notifications?

Do you spend time mindlessly scrolling through your newsfeed and you don't know why?

You may have unconsciously rewired the reward center of your brain to crave the chemical dump that social media stimulates.

"Dopamine, the main chemical involved in addiction, is secreted from certain nerve tracts in the brain when we engage in a rewarding experience."[3] Stanford psychiatrist Anna Lembke says that checking our social media accounts is especially addictive because our bodies are made to crave human connection. Social media provides a fake, overstimulating version of community, which causes your brain to secrete large amounts of dopamine. "Just as the hypodermic needle is the delivery mechanism for drugs like heroin, the smartphone is the modern-day hypodermic needle, delivering digital dopamine for a wired generation."[4]

This may sound like hyperbole, but social media corporations admittedly use this biological component to manipulate users to log in more often and stay on longer. "Platforms like Facebook, Snapchat, and Instagram leverage the very same neural circuitry used by slot machines and cocaine to keep us using their products as much as possible."[5]

The individuals responsible for writing these algorithms must know what they're doing.

In 2018, the average American touched their phone screen 2,600 times a day.(6)

This means you may have already tapped your phone hoping for a "hit" of happiness thousands of times today. It's like we're continuously trying to "draw" contentment from a digital well with our fingers.

When I observe people in public, constantly pecking away at their phones, I am reminded of a character from Greek mythology named Sisyphus. As a punishment, poor Sisyphus is doomed to roll a boulder up a hill for all eternity. Every time he nears the top, his burden tumbles back to the bottom and he is forced to repeat the pointless process. This is us as our fingers dance endlessly across our screens. We are "rolling our boulders," believing that if we just watch enough *Tik Tok* videos, get just enough likes, we will eventually crest the hill of happiness. Like cursed Sysiphus, we will find that this pinnacle of digitally-generated peace is merely an illusion.

There is no amount of screen taps that will fill the God-deep desires of the human soul. By returning over and over to so shallow a well, we are actually making ourselves thirstier. Neuroscience shows us that when we constantly seek out our phones for a shot of dopamine, we throw our brains out of balance. Our pleasure centers work like see-saws. In our constant quest to go *higher*, we also begin to dip *lower*. "Each time the thing becomes less enjoyable, but we eventually become dependent on those stimuli to keep functioning. We spiral into a joy-seeking abyss."(7)

This is the blueprint for addiction —we train our brains to believe we need a certain something other than God to be happy. Through our overindulgence we have made it impossible to feel contentment without the constant stimulation of our phones. Despite our ability to get free, infinite "hits' from our phone whenever we want, society is more depressed than ever.(8) Our attempts to fuel our happiness by synthetic community have failed and will continue to fail. As C.S. Lewis says, "God designed the human machine to run on Himself. He Himself is the fuel our spirits were designed to feed on. There is no other. That is why it is just no good asking God to make us happy in our own way…God cannot give us a happiness and peace apart from Himself, because it is not there. There is no such thing."(9)

Social media addiction is so dangerous because it keeps us from coming to the one Well that will never run dry. I can just picture Christ snatching my phone from my hand and pointing at its glowing screen, "Everyone who drinks of this water will be thirsty again"(John 4:13). He then pulls my now empty fingers into His own and says, "But whoever drinks of the water I will give him will never be thirsty again. The water that I will give him will become in him a spring of water welling up to eternal life" (John 4:14).

When we begin to treat our phones like they are responsible for maintaining our happiness, we fall prey to the most lethal lie of all   "We lose confidence that Christ really can satisfy me."(10) The battle for our attention is so important because, "There's no greater catastrophic loss imaginable to a soul than to grow weary of Christ."(11)

Have you noticed your soul growing numb towards the things of God? Does the thought of the cross still pull on your heart as it did at the beginning? Perhaps you have unintentionally allowed your soul to "drift" from the Living God, not by cycles of willful sin, but simply by not paying attention to Him. Hebrew 2:1 says, "Therefore, we must pay much closer attention to what we have heard, lest we drift away from it." Most of us don't purposefully reset our sails and begin to paddle away from Christ, we simply let our minds and our hearts drift from Him when we set our sights on the digital world instead of the Presence of God. "Affectional drift away from Christ (in our hearts) is caused by attentional drift away from Christ."(12)

Don't fall for the lie that your attention isn't a valuable commodity. If our attention directs our affections, it's the most precious gift we have to give.

Our social media addiction is not just restructuring our minds, it's rewiring our loves.

I felt foolish and enthralled and thrilled all at the same time when I read Dane Ortland's description of treasuring Christ with our minds. He says we should, "Romance the heart of Jesus."(13) His use of the word, "romance" had my heart skipping a beat. *Why had I not thought of it this way before?*

When you're in love with someone, the entire landscape of your mind shifts. No one has to tell you to think about your significant other. Your mind unconsciously returns over and over to all the things you love and admire about him: the way his hair falls across his forehead, the sound of his laugh, the kind way he treated a stranger. As you meditate on all his amazing qualities, your love for him grows. On the outside, you may be completing ordinary tasks, but on the inside, your mind has become a sanctuary for kindling romance. What began as a small spark has grown into a wildfire of desire and affection, fueled by the weight of your attention. All you can think about is the next occasion when you two will be able to spend time together.

What would happen if we chose to give the gift our attention to Christ? Our forever Bridegroom is more lovely, more fascinating, more wonderful, than any human lover and the ONLY ONE beautiful enough to captivate us forever. What would happen if we took the "spark" of the Word He has revealed to us and let it kindle in our hearts all throughout the day? What would happen if we ran over His qualities, His goodness, His promises like we replay the things we admire about our earthly loves?

If we don't get a case of the spiritual butterflies when we think about Jesus, it's not because He has become less lovely, *it's because we've stopped really looking at Him.*

Maybe we haven't been "romancing" immoral things, but in giving the gift of our attention to things that don't really matter, we have unconsciously snuffed out our love for Christ. We might not think about our phones as our "lovers," but that's what they become when we allow them to take Christ's rightful place in our hearts.

When the people of Israel would turn away from God and begin to worship the gods of their enemies, our Father didn't call it a "bad habit" they should try to break, he called it adultery. "Like a wife who commits adultery, Israel has worshiped other gods on every hill and under every green tree"(Jeremiah 3:6b). We may not be bowing down and offering sacrifices to our smart phones, but when we ask them to do things for us that only God do, we commit idolatry. *Yikes!*

Author Sarah Clarkson noticed a growing "white noise" in her mind, and decided to embark on a Facebook fast one summer. (14) As she tuned out the digital world, she noticed a restoration of focus and clarity. "In the silence that grew. I slowed, and an inner space was forged within me from which I looked out on the world, able to weigh my thoughts, consider my choices, and know my emotions before the press of the outer world provoked me into action."(15)

When Clarkson observed that, "an inner space was forged within," her, this was true both physically and metaphorically. Do you know that our thoughts cause actual, physical changes in our brains? Our minds are crisscrossed with trillions of little highways called, "neural pathways." These mental routes can be compared to hiking trails.(16) Every time we think, it's as if the "feet" of our thoughts travel down a neural pathway. The more often we fixate on a certain subject, or repeat a behavior, the deeper and more worn the neural pathway becomes. Since our minds would rather choose a clean, cut trail than an uncharted jungle, our brains will default to traversing the most well, worn pathways. Over time, our habits create such deep grooves that it becomes difficult to take another route and establish a new pattern of behavior. Have you ever reached for your phone without even realizing it? Maybe you have traveled down the "check Facebook" lane so many times that it looks more like the Grand Canyon than a hiking trail.

The good news is that no matter our age, or how long we've been cutting the wrong sorts of trails, our minds are capable of change. We *can* cut new pathways. Old, abandoned pathways *can* be re-opened through conscious effort.

When Clarkson made the difficult decision to unplug, her mind was forced to forge new paths to find stimulation and satisfaction. Since reading her account I have been prayerfully attempting to navigate through each day like a woman on an expedition towards the heart of Christ. With my every thought, I can even either slip-and-slide into the white noise of entertainment, or I can carve out a deeper space for me and Jesus. I can enlarge our sanctuary, create a wider space for our love to grow.

If you were to get an aerial view of my mind, I would want you to see a roadmap of trails all leading towards Christ. I want the highways of my heart to tell the story of someone seeking the eternal.

When Clarkson remade the landscape of her heart, she found that she no longer wanted to escape from reality into the world of social media. Instead, she now wanted to bring the reality of the Kingdom into the world around her. "No room is just space. No hour is meaningless. No meal is mere sustenance. Every rhythm and atom of existence are spaces in which the Kingdom can come, in which the story of God's love can be told anew, in which the stuff of life can be turned marvelously into love."(17)

I will admit to using my phone as a way to emotionally escape from a difficult parenting situation or stressful ordeal. It's so much easier to think about my friend's new puppy than to think about how my dog just tipped over the trashcans and dragged their contents all over the yard. It's easier to accept the "likes" of people through a screen than to deal with a severed relationship at work. It's so much more pleasant to look at interior design on Pinterest than to face the upheaval of my own living room.

God's Word reminds me that when I run away from hard situations, I actually run away from Jesus. He wants to use the trials of this life, big and small, to shape us into His Son.
"Count it all joy, my brothers, when you meet trials of various kinds, for you know that the testing of your faith produces steadfastness. And let steadfastness have its full effect, that you may be perfect and complete, lacking in nothing" (James 1:2-4).

Most of the time, I would rather be immature and watch Facebook reels than be a grown up who has to do the dishes. Why would I choose to do the hard thing when the easy thing is free and waiting for me right at my fingertips?

Who would choose to use their strength to pick up a cross when they could use it to scroll through pixelated paradise?

People who know that Jesus is better than anything else, *that's who!*

People who know that we don't get Christ when we try to escape from all the hard or boring stuff.

His heart beats through ours when we walk right into the mess and lay our lives down. I need to post this on my wall, on my phone wallpaper, hang it on my mirror —

Don't drop your cross to pick up your phone.

Don't let the allure of the digital world dampen your view of reality. Our phones are like free passports to the cybernetic universe. This access to everywhere will convince us that somewhere, anywhere out there must be better than right here.

There is no better place on earth than right where you are, fully surrendered to Christ.

Jesus meets us in the moment.

Let Him be your escape. We don't need to mentally check into a fantasy world to be content. The Truth is far better than our wildest imaginations.

Let's reprogram our instincts to reach for Christ.

Let's retrain our minds to *need what we really need.*

Let me be careful to clarify that I am not advocating for the boycotting of smartphones and a total abandonment of social media.

I think our withdrawal from the online culture would be a devastating blow for the Kingdom.

The realm of social media is one of the biggest missions field in our culture. Much of my personal ministry would not be possible without the connections I have made through online community. We may need to periodically fast from our phones, but wise and thoughtful engagement with social media can be good and productive. Since we are pre-programmed to slide down the trail of addiction, we need to make a plan beforehand to keep us on track.

In this chart, I have given some practical suggestions for "carving a new path" with our online engagement.

It's okay to look at pretty paint colors on Pinterest. It's okay to catch up with high school friends. It's ok to laugh at funny videos.

Just don't allow the online world be your source of life.

Don't go there to be fed.

Go there to *feed others* with the love of Jesus.

Social Media Detox Plan

SIMPLIFY INPUTS

- Are you active on Twitter, Facebook, Tik Tok, Instagram etc.? Pick one or two. It's hard to be intentional on so many platforms. Go deep, not wide.

GIVE YOUR DEVICE A BEDTIME AND A WAKE-UP TIME

- Reserve your first and last hours for in-person interaction and time in the Word. Kind of like intermittent fasting, but with your phone.

TAKE A MEDIA FAST

Pick one day a week to silence all devices. If you want to go big, fast for a whole week or more.

SET LIMITS

- Force yourself to set a timer before opening an app, stick with it.
- Choose to watch only 3 random videos a day

CHOOSE REPLACEMENTS

- Research and buy some good books. Download the Kindle app.
- Start your day with the "First 5" app or the "She Reads Truth" app to start your day with the Word

Social Media
MY PERSONALIZED DETOX PLAN

WRITE IT DOWN!!!!!!
HOW WILL YOU BE INTENTIONAL TO USE SOCIAL MEDIA TO FEED OTHERS INSTEAD OF FEEDING YOURSELF USELESS INFORMATION?

TIME WITH THE LORD IS NOT A MAGIC PILL, A FORMULA,
NOT A DUTY, CERTAINLY NOT A "EASY BUTTON," AND NOT
AKIN TO BURNING INCENSE TO APPEASE A DISTANT GOD;
IT'S SIMPLY WHAT WE WERE CREATED FOR --
A RELATIONSHIP WITH HIM.

-Ruth Chou Simons

Why Process Matters

Before Christ left earth, He promised the disciples He would send a Helper who would, "guide you into all truth"(John 16:13). Though His followers would no longer be able to hear His words with their physical ears, the Holy Spirit would soon speak into their hearts and, "glorify Me by taking from what is Mine and disclosing it to you" (John 16:14).

This same Spirit indwells believers today and "illuminates the brilliance and depth of God's Word to us."(1) If Christians have 24/7, personal access to the Author of the Bible, then why should we have to worry about proper process when studying Scripture?

Shouldn't we just be able to glance at the words and instantly ascertain their meaning? Won't the Holy Spirit just correct us if we have the wrong interpretation of a certain passage?

The Bible also makes it clear that the presence of the Holy Spirit does not excuse us from learning how to accurately interpret the Word.

In Hebrews 5:13, Paul criticizes his readers for remaining "unskilled in the Word of righteousness."

In 2 Timothy 2:15, Paul tells Timothy, "Do your best to present yourself to God as one approved, a worker who has no need to be ashamed, rightly handling the word of Truth. "

When we receive the Holy Spirit, we are not automatically downloaded with the ability to engage productively with Scripture. Proper interpretation is a learned skill. This also helps us to understand why wonderful, Godly men and women disagree on the correct interpretation of various passages of Scripture.

"The Holy Spirit is not a 'cure-all' for poor interpretation. He does not automatically reverse the consequences of violating hermeneutical principles."(2)

This means that a person with a very sincere love for Christ is still at risk of misinterpreting Scripture.

"He is walking with God, but he fails to obey the basic laws of interpretation; so he is wrong, and the Holy Spirit does not automatically correct him."(3)

This should not erode our confidence as we approach the Word, but cause us to pay closer attention to our process, or our "exegesis" of the text. It should also cause us to steer clear of teachers who dismiss the need for careful study and claim that the Spirit led them to a "new" understanding of Scripture. Such claims are the recipe for disaster and a falling away from the Truth.

We learned earlier that accurate information about God is foundational for cultivating intimacy with Him. It is therefore crucial that we learn to approach the Word in a way that leads to a true understanding of God's intended message.

> *Exegesis is the furthest thing from pedantry; exegesis is an act of love. It is loving the one enough who speaks the words to get the words right. It is respecting the words enough to use every means we have to get the words right. Exegesis is loving God enough to stop and listen carefully to what He says. God has provided us with these scriptures that present us with His Word. Loving God means loving both what God speaks to us and the way God speaks to us.... Lovers savor the words, relishing every nuance of what is said and written. (4)*

Don't panic! Process isn't just for professionals! You don't need to attend seminary to study Scripture for yourself.

God would not have promised that we could seek Him and find Him if He had placed understanding out of our reach. Before we talk about the *right* way to approach Bible study, I am going to highlight some of the ways we should avoid.

I would wager that all Christians have engaged in these improper methods at some point. I know I have used them all more frequently and more recently than I would like to admit.

HOW NOT TO STUDY THE BIBLE

THE FORTUNE COOKIE

We've all done it. We come to the Word with no direction and no game plan; so we close our eyes, flop our Bible open, and let our finger fall randomly onto a page. We may even make a strange humming sound or twirl our finger in the air before bringing it down to add extra dramatic flair. In this approach to Scripture, we treat God like some sort of Cosmic Magic Eight Ball. (5) We believe that our fingers will be divinely guided to the pre-ordained passage which will give us the enlightenment we need for the day ahead.

The problem -- the Bible is not designed to function like a fortune cookie. We aren't meant to just crack it open and find a random verse to treat like a horoscope. When we do this, we leave ourselves open to dangerous misinterpretation and misapplication of the text.

There's a famous story about a man who tried this method and opened to the passage which reads, "And Judas went and hanged himself." Obviously, God did not intend for this poor man to re-enact this tragic scenario.

This does not mean that God never guides us to specific passages of Scripture. I have innumerable memories of times when He brought me to just the right verse at just the right time. In most instances, however, these divine lifelines did not come through a random, "pinch your eyes shut and point" encounter.

THE OVERACHIEVER

I taught myself how to speed read when I was a senior in high school. I figured it would be a helpful skill to have in college.

I was right.

I daily regret this decision.

Though speed reading was very handy for pulling out relevant information in dense, academic texts, this habit has hampered my ability to slow down and appreciate the beauty of the language in any physical book. It drains all the color out of novels and if I'm not careful, it can cause me to miss the meaning tucked inside Bible passages. The Scriptures weren't meant for speed; they were meant for savoring. You might be a Bible overachiever if you are more interested in the *quantity* of the Word you intake, than you are in the *quality* of your understanding.

An example of a Biblical overachiever may be someone who engages in a yearly Bible reading plan. There is absolutely nothing wrong with reading the Bible in this way, however, it becomes problematic when you are intaking more than you can properly digest. If you read four chapters today, but you don't really absorb any of it, you haven't "achieved" anything. It is better to sit and savor four verses than to read an entire book and retain none of the information.

GOLDEN CORRAL

Covid took many things from us. One of these casualties was the local Golden Corral. I've never been to Disney World, but I am pretty sure that going to Golden Corral as a five-year-old is an equivalent experience to visiting the Magic Kingdom.

There was an unlimited amount of food, and you could eat *whatever you wanted*!

So what does every kindergartner do? They run straight to the nacho and dessert bar and cover their plate with cheese dip and sprinkle-covered ice cream!!! *Am I right or am I right!?*

Some of us approach the Bible like I approached the chocolate fondue fountain at Golden Corral. We treat the Bible like a buffet and only go for the sweet, fluffy stuff that's easy to understand and digest. We only choose to "eat" passages that are not going to cause any pain or conviction. We think the Bible is meant to be comfort food and to eat solely to "feel good."

When we refuse to acknowledge the parts of God's character that make us uncomfortable, we are essentially creating our own version of God. Tim Keller explains the danger of this approach, "A Jesus that fits in with what you think Jesus should be like can't challenge you, can't convict you, therefore can't really change you or transform you."(6)

When you skip over the hard chunks of the Bible, you skip over crucial opportunities for growth.

THEOLOGIAN IDOL

Much like *American Idol*, this approach describes believers who adore a preacher's voice and become an avid fan of his theology. It is right and wise to seek Godly teaching, but we should be careful not to read Godly literature to the neglect of reading Scripture. Listening to great preaching cannot replace personal, face-to-face time with the Word. "If you can quote John Piper more than the Apostle Paul, we have a problem."(7)

Lysa Terkheurst says this method is like a person who attends a banquet, intently watches other guests enjoy their food, but refuses to fix their own plate. "You will not be nourished until you actually ingest and digest it for yourself. The same is true for Scripture. You must take in God's Word for yourself."(8)

Speaking of food, we've finally arrived at the part of the book you've all been waiting for! Now that we've explored some ineffective methods of Bible study, let's learn how to do it right! Get ready to pick up your "fork" and "knife" and eat the Word for yourself!

but one thing is necessary. Mary has chosen the good portion, which will not be taken away from her Luke 10:42 but one thing is necessary. Mary has chosen the good portion, which will not be taken away from her Luke 10:42 but one thing is necessary. Mary has chosen the good portion, which will not be taken away from her Luke 10:42 but one thing is necessary. Mary has chosen the good portion, which will not be taken away from her Luke 10:42 but one thing is necessary. Mary has chosen the good portion, which will not be taken away from her Luke 10:42 but one thing is necessary. Mary has chosen the good portion, which will not be taken away from her Luke 10:42 but one thing is necessary. Mary has chosen the good portion, which will not be taken away from her Luke 10:42 but one thing is necessary. Mary has chosen the good portion, which will not be taken away from her Luke 10:42 but one thing is necessary. Mary has chosen the good portion, which will not be taken away from her Luke 10:42 but one thing is necessary. Mary has chosen the good portion, which will not be taken away from her Luke 10:42 but one thing is necessary. Mary has chosen the good portion, which will not be taken away from her Luke 10:42 but one thing is necessary. Mary has chosen the good portion, which will not be taken away from her Luke 10:42 but one thing is necessary. Mary has chosen the good portion, which will not be taken away from her Luke 10:42 but one thing is necessary. Mary has chosen the good portion, which will not be taken away from her Luke 10:42 but one thing is necessary. Mary has chosen the good portion, which will not be taken away from her Luke 10:42 but one thing is necessary. Mary has chosen the good portion, which will not be taken away from her Luke 10:42 but one thing is necessary. Mary has chosen the good portion, which will not be taken away from her Luke

IN THE SECRET
IN THE QUIET PLACE
IN THE STILLNESS
YOU ARE THERE
IN THE SECRET
IN THE QUIET HOUR I WAIT
ONLY FOR YOU
CAUSE, I WANT TO KNOW YOU MORE

-Chris Tomlin

How To Read the Bible

Wooooooo!!!

Are you excited yet!?

My husband thinks I use the word, "Woooo" rather obsessively and likes to tease me about it. If there ever was a moment for "wooing," this is it!!! Just picture me jumping up and down and pounding my fists in the air. You can join me in this imaginary party if you would like!

WOOOOOO!!

Sorry, can't help myself.

In this section, we will show you our design template for personal Bible study, and walk you through an example study.

Is this the only way you can study the Bible?

Absolutely not.

Do you have to do every single step we outline in the exact way we describe?

Nope.

Do we hope that this helps you find the rhythm that works for you and give you the tools you need to encounter Jesus for yourself in the secret place!?

Yes! Yes! And more yes!

Before we open our Bibles, I believe it is crucial to pause and take some time to posture our hearts before Heaven. You will find the first section in our journal template is entitled, "Pour it out." This is where we take our "jars of perfume" – all the things that have been weighing heavy on our hearts, all the little distractions, the tug of the to-do list – and we choose to push pause and pour them out on the feet of Christ. You have may have to do some physical as well as mental rearranging. Maybe you need to put your phone in another room, or go to a space where you're not going to be constantly distracted by clutter or things that need cleaned or organized. The temptation to exchange a small "good" thing for the "best" thing is real. If I am in a room that needs cleaning, it is very hard for my mind to relax and enjoy Jesus.

A few minutes ago, I stood up from the computer, grabbed my broom, and swept up a dirty spot without even realizing I had done it. *#mombrain* Maybe you need to go outside or sit by a window, so you can fix your eyes on the beauty of God's creation. Put yourself in the location that will best set you up for success.

Sometimes, finding the "perfect" spot won't be possible. You might be in your car during lunch break. You might be laying on the floor beside your child's crib with your head is on a stuffed elephant and your feet are on a pile of matchbox cars -- that's ok too. You don't have to be in the perfect place to meet Jesus. Remember, we serve a God who meets us wherever we are.

Come before Heaven and thank the Father for the unparalleled gift of being able to communicate with Him. Ask Him to open your eyes to the life-changing truths found in His Word.

Acknowledge your weakness and your need for Him to speak.
If you are still dealing with mental clutter, stop and write it down in the "Pour It Out" section. Remember something you need to put on your grocery list? *Write it down*. Realize you need to shoot someone a text? Write it down so you won't forget. If things pop into your mind throughout your study, you can continue to lay them down in the "Pour It Out" box. It's a simple surrender that shows you are entrusting your life into the loving hands of the Father. He promises that when we seek Him first, He will take care of all the other little details of life (Matthew 6:33). The type of study we will be exploring is called "Inductive Bible Study" and is broken down into three sections--

OBSERVATION
WHAT HAPPENED?

INTERPRETATION
WHY DOES THIS MATTER?

APPLICATION
WHAT DOES THIS TELL ME ABOUT GOD AND HOW SHOULD THIS CHANGE ME?

Though the term, "inductive" may be new to you, it's actually a process your mind is very familiar with. Whether or not we are aware of it, the human mind moves through these three steps everyday to interpret and navigate through reality. We see what's happening around us, understand what it means, and react appropriately.

EXAMPLE #1:

Observation: We see the traffic light turn red.

Interpretation: We understand that are in danger of being hit by oncoming traffic.

Application: We lower our foot and hit the brake.

EXAMPLE #2:

Observation: We hear our infant crying,

Interpretation: We realize it's been two hours since his last meal and our sweet baby is probably hungry.

Application: We feed her.

To give a simplified Biblical example let's go to the feeding of the five thousand found in Mark 14.

Observation: Jesus miraculously multiplies one child's small lunch to feed a crowd of over five thousand people.

Interpretation: Jesus has power over the natural world and can use anything He wants to provide for His children.

Application: I should not fear because God will provide for me no matter how bleak the situation looks. He can take my little and turn it into a lot.

Though our minds flow through this progression naturally, it is crucial to break down and analyze each step when we are interpreting something as complex as a Biblical text.

Each step in the inductive process builds on the others. We must build a firm foundation of observation and interpretation if we hope to have a stable and accurate application.

STEP #1...OBSERVATION

When we observe Scripture, we are asking the basic question, "What is happening?"

As we learned in "See The Bigger Story," it is crucial that we understand the context of a passage of Scripture if we are to truly apprehend God's intended message. Though the books you were assigned to read in high school weren't divinely inspired, some of the tactics you used to study great works of literature can and should be applied when studying your Bible.

Do these questions sound familiar?

WHO? WHAT? WHEN? WHERE? WHY? HOW?

You're going to ask the "Bible" version of these questions in the observation portion. These questions are different when you are examining a book of the Bible than when you are examining a passage of Scripture within that book.

My sister is a speech pathologist. One of her strategies when working with younger children is to do a "book walk-through." I love the mental image of walking through a book to get an overarching grasp of its content. Asking the "W's" for books of the Bible is a great way to do this.

So let's "walk through" Luke together.

Though you don't have to write the answer to these questions down every time you crack open your Bible, it's important that you have this information in the back of your mind as you approach the text.

You may already be an expert on Luke, but for example's sake, let's pretend you never heard of the guy.

Here's a handy chart you can reference while doing your studies to help you remember the "5 W's of Books"

Observation

THE 5 W'S OF BOOKS

WHO?
WHO WROTE THIS BOOK?
TO WHOM WAS IT WRITTEN?

WHAT?
IN WHAT STYLE WAS THIS BOOK WRITTEN?

WHEN?
WHEN WAS THIS BOOK WRITTEN?
(IN CHRONOLOGICAL TERMS &
IN THE BIGGER STORY OF SCRIPTURE)

WHERE?
WHERE WAS THE ACTION HAPPENING?

WHY?
WHY WAS THIS BOOK WRITTEN?

Don't stress. If you have a study Bible, the answers to all of these questions should be found at the beginning of each book.

If you don't have a study Bible, there are tons of wonderful, free online resources that provide access to articles, books, and charts with this information. My go-to is *blueletterbible.org*, but there are dozens of others. We have included a resource list in the back of this book with some helpful suggestions on various tools you can use in your quest to increase your Biblical literacy. This list is by no means exhaustive, but we hope it will aid your search and connect you with the knowledge you need to grow.

Who—Who wrote Luke?
As you may have guessed, Luke was written by Luke. The author was a physician who traveled with the Apostle Paul. Luke is known for his attention to detail and has a reputation as a meticulous historian and intellectual. Interestingly, Luke was not Jewish and did not witness the events he recorded in the book firsthand. Instead, he writes his Gospel based on the testimony of eyewitness accounts.

What— In what style was Luke written?
Books of the Bible have historically been categorized into eight major genres. Understanding the style of each book is helpful in determining how best to interpret the text.
For instance -- you wouldn't want to interpret poetry as a historic event, or a historic event as a metaphor. Here are some reference charts to help explain each of the genres, and the books which fall into these categories.

Biblical Genres
Books

NARRATIVE

OLD TESTAMENT:
- GENESIS, EXODUS, NUMBERS, DEUTERONOMY, JOSHUA, JUDGES, RUTH, 1&2 SAMUEL, 1&2 KINGS, 1&2 CHRONICLES, EZRA, NEHEMIAH, ESTHER, PARTS OF JOB AND THE PROPHETS

NEW TESTAMENT:
- MATTHEW, MARK, LUKE, JOHN, ACTS

THE LAW

OLD TESTAMENT:
- LEVITICUS
- PARTS OF EXODUS, NUMBERS, & DEUTERONOMY

POETRY

OLD TESTAMENT:
- PSALMS
- SONG OF SOLOMON
- LAMENTATIONS
- PARTS OF OT NARRATIVES

WISDOM

OLD TESTAMENT:
- PROVERBS
- JOB
- ECCLESIASTES

PROPHECY

OLD TESTAMENT:
MAJOR PROPHETS-
- ISAIAH, JEREMIAH, EZEKIEL, DANIEL

MINOR PROPHETS-
- HOSEA, JOEL, AMOS, OBADIAH, JONAH, MICAH, NAHUM, HABBAKUK, ZEPHANIAH, HAGGAI, ZECHARIAH, MALACHI

APOCALYPTIC

OLD TESTAMENT:
- PARTS OF ISAIAH, JEREMIAH, EZEKIEL, JOEL, DANIEL

NEW TESTAMENT:
- MATTHEW 24-25, MARK 13, 2 THESSALONIANS 2
- ALL OF REVELATION

GOSPELS

NEW TESTAMENT:
- MATTHEW
- MARK
- LUKE
- JOHN

EPISTLES

NEW TESTAMENT:
- ROMANS, 1&2 CORINTHIANS, GALATIANS, EPHESIANS, COLOSSIANS, 1&2 THESSALONIANS, 1&2 TIMOTHY, TITUS, PHILEMON, 1&2 PETER, JAMES, 1,2,&3 JOHN, JUDE, HEBREWS

Biblical Genres
Descriptions

NARRATIVE

- Factual accounts of real events
- Not to be understood as legend or fable
- These are stories about real people encountering a real God

THE LAW

- Laws given by God to the nation of Israel. Part of the establishment of his covenant with them as his chosen people.
- <u>3 types of law</u>:
  - Moral
  - Ceremonial
  - Judicial

POETRY

- Hebrew poetry which may include metaphor, symbolism, parallel structure, and even prophecy.
- Some poems were song lyrics and even include the instruments which were to be played

WISDOM

- Practical wisdom given to aid the reader in navigating successfully through life.

PROPHECY

- Prophets served as God's mouthpiece and revealed messages to the people of Israel, visions, and glimpses into the future.
- Some prophecy is easy to interpret, others use symbolic language

APOCALYPTIC

- These writings use symbolic language to describe end-time events

GOSPELS

- Historical narrative which records the events of Christ's life while he was on earth.

EPISTLES

<u>New Testament</u>:
- Romans, 1 & 2 Corinthians, Galatians, Ephesians, Colossians, 1 & 2 Thessalonians, 1-2 Timothy, Titus, Philemon, 1 & 2 Peter, James, 1-3 John, Jude, Hebrews

When — When was Luke written? Where does it fall in the grander story of Scripture?
Around 62 AD, about 30 years after Jesus' death. If we look at the metanarrative of Scripture, we find that these events occur briefly before Christ bought our redemption on the cross.

Where —Where was the action in Luke happening?
The events in this book take place in Israel during the life of Christ.

Why —Why was Luke written?
Luke addressed this book to an unknown friend named Theophilus. Though he addressed his writing to a single person, it was meant to reach a broader audience.

Now that we've "walked through" Luke, let's get ready to dig into our text for today. Before we begin, here are the five W's to have in your mind as you read.

Observation

THE 5 W'S OF TEXT

WHO?
WHO ARE THE CHARACTERS IN THIS PASSAGE? WHO IS SPEAKING?

WHAT?
WHAT HAPPENED IN THIS PASSAGE?

WHEN?
WHEN IS THE ACTION OCCURRING? BOTH WITHIN THE GRANDER STORY AND WITHIN THE BOOK ITSELF?

WHERE?
WHERE IS THE ACTION OCCURRING?

WHY/HOW?
(THESE ARE SAVED FOR INTERPRETATION)

Not only do we want to read with our eyes primed for the answers to "W" questions, we want to be on the hunt for certain sorts of words and phrases that can help us better understand the passage.

It's a lot of fun when you approach it like a treasure hunt!

Key Words & Phrases

- USED MULTIPLE TIMES
- ESSENTIAL TO THE MEANING OF THE TEXT
- ANYTHING THAT STRIKES YOUR CURIOSITY AND YOU HAVE A QUESTION ABOUT

Transitional Phrases

- THEREFORE, FINALLY, IN CONCLUSION, BECAUSE, SO, ETC..
- THESE PHRASES ARE BASICALLY SHOUTING, "PAY ATTENTION TO ME!" THIS IS WHERE THE "WHY" HAPPENS

Contrasts & Comparisons

- GOD IS LIKE, MAN IS LIKE
- RATHER, INSTEAD, BUT, WHEREAS

Expressions Of Time

- AFTER, A LITTLE WHILE, ETERNAL, BEFORE, FOREVER AND EVER

Some people like to go all out and use different colored highlighters to mark their key words and phrases. I am not personally that organized, but if you want to whip out your pencil pouch, you go right ahead!

Now that you know what you're looking for, why don't you whip out your Bibles and read our chosen portion, Luke 10:38-42, for yourself.

Let's go through what we've found in our "treasure hunt" together.

Who- Who are the characters in this passage?
Mary and Martha- Sisters who are personal friends with Christ. It appears that their house was a common stop for Jesus and His disciples when they traveled through the area.
Jesus-Creator of the universe. King of all Kings. Only Son of God. Lamb slain before the foundation of the world. My favorite Character of all time.

What- Jesus visits the house of Martha and Mary. While Martha is busy preparing dinner, Mary chooses to sit and listen to Jesus teach. This enrages Martha, who asks Jesus to command her to help in the kitchen. Jesus surprises Martha by refusing her request and explaining that Mary is the one who has chosen wisely.

When- This event occurred at the height of Christ's ministry. He was traveling, preaching, and performing miracles. By this point He had gathered a large following as well as a host of enemies.

Where- At the house of Mary, Martha, and Lazarus, in the little town of Bethany located on the outskirts of Jerusalem. Jesus would often stay there when visiting the Holy City.

KEY WORDS:
v. 40 -"distracted"
v.42- "one thing is necessary"
v.42 -"the Good Portion"

NO TRANSITIONAL PHRASES OR EXPRESSIONS OF TIME

COMPARISON/CONTRASTS:
v39-40 -"but, Martha was distracted with much serving."
v 41 -"But the Lord answered her..."
v.42 -"But one thing is necessary."

Keyword Research

It is not necessary to do additional research on all keywords. Occasionally, however, you may find a word that piques your curiosity. It's never been easier to do your own simple, yet fruitful word study. I typically use *blueletterbible.org* for help in this investigation. Simply choose the version of the Bible you are currently using, then type in your chosen passage.

Once you select "tools," you will have access to such resources as the Strong's definition of the term, an outline of its Biblical usage, a Greek Lexicon (which is basically a fancy term for a Greek dictionary), and a list of other places this phrase has been used in Scripture.

Since we are English speakers, it can also be helpful to look up keywords in an English dictionary. The translators worked very hard to select words that would convey the original author's meaning. When we look at the English definition, we may actually gain a deeper understanding of the Greek definition.

My favorite thing to do with key words is to cross reference their use in other parts of Scripture. Once we begin cross-referencing, we have officially crossed over into the "Interpretation" section.

WOOOOOOOOOOO!!! (You knew I had to do it.)

In our devotional template, we have lumped the Observation and Interpretation sections together. Many people, including myself, find that observation bleeds automatically into interpretation. For these people, physically separating the two processes on paper can actually be counterproductive. We want you to have the freedom to write as the Spirit moves. As you become more familiar with inductive study and find that your mind works better by separating the two ideas, please draw yourself a big fat line down the middle of the Observation/Interpretation box. Make it your own!

We have now officially circled back to our "Why" and our "How" questions.

WHY?

Why does this matter?
What does it mean?

We can answer the "Why" question by asking the "How" question.

HOW?

"How would the original hearers have understood this?"

Interpretation
Cheat Sheet

WHY?
- Why does this matter?

HOW?
How would the original recipients have understood this?

CROSS-REFERENCE
- Where have similar themes or stories been discussed elsewhere in the Bible?
- "Let scripture interpret scripture."

TRANSLATION
- Read the same passage in a different translation

RESOURCES
- Footnotes, commentaries, reference books, etc.

Tips For Interpretation

-USE SCRIPTURE TO INTERPRET SCRIPTURE.

-In your study Bible, you will notice tiny numbers or letters sprinkled throughout your text and throughout the margins. These will lead you to other instances in the Word where this same word or phrase has been used. Maybe this same story has been used in another Gospel, but with added detail. Maybe this is a direct fulfillment of prophecy. Maybe the author is quoting a Psalm. Cross-referencing is one of the best ways to discover a text's richest, fullest meaning.

-Remember -- *Scripture will never contradict Scripture*. A clear truth that you find in one place will never contradict a statement found elsewhere. This should keep us from basing our doctrine on a single, obscure, passage of Scripture. If scholars argue over the meaning of a Scripture, you probably shouldn't base your whole theology on it. Base your core beliefs on what is clear.

-INTERPRET LITERALLY-

Most of the time, the meaning of a passage of Scripture is clear and straightforward. You can get into big trouble looking for a hidden message in every verse. If there is another layer of meaning, it will become apparent through careful study. Obviously, there are some exceptions, like books of prophecy such as Revelation. This is why it's so important to be familiar with the genres of Scripture, and to interpret according to that style.

-RESOURCES-

Not all passages of Scripture will require additional cultural or historical background information in order to fully understand. If there is relevant information that might change the interpretation of the passage, it will normally be included in the footnotes section of your study Bible. I am extremely fascinated with Israeli culture, and I find that learning more about the world of the Bible gives so much texture and color to the Scripture as I'm reading it. The Word comes alive in a whole new way when we understand it through its proper cultural and historic lens. I have included some of my resources on this subject in the resource section at the back of this book.

Time to dive into our interpretation!

WOOOOOOOOOOOOOOOOOOOOOOO!!!!!!! (Wow! I may actually have a problem here.)

Before we begin, let me clarify that the goal of biblical interpretation is not human brilliance. Human intelligence or creativity has nothing to do with knowing our Creator. Isn't our King just amazing? Gender, race, IQ, education, social status -- none of it matters in the pursuit of God. Jesus is equally available to everyone. He is just as available to you as He was to Billy Graham, the Apostle Paul, and Simon Peter. **Knowing God is not about "smart," it's about "heart."**

When we begin to interpret, we are simply trying to be faithful to what God was trying to communicate to us through this text. We don't have to make anything up or use impressive sounding words. We are *not* going to impress God with our interpretation of Scripture.

It's not about what we bring to the table. It's about what's *already being served* at the table.

If there's any brilliance happening during our interpretation, it's what God has *already* said. This world does not need more of my words, *it needs more of His words.*

I also want to point out that I have had a long, long time to chew on this interpretation. I have been intently studying this passage of Scripture for almost a year now. Though we won't normally spend a year dissecting a single passage, it's *okay to take your time with Scripture.* This is the first time I've fixated so long on a single story, but I have previously spent weeks or longer on a single chapter or book of the Bible, attempting to pull all the marrow out of its meaning. Don't feel pressured to fill out an entire journal page each day. It might take you a week to do one study.

You also shouldn't feel pressured to fill up the entirety of each journal page with text. Maybe your takeaway is one sentence long, but it changes you forever.

There are also going to be times when you look at a passage of Scripture, maybe even a single verse, and you are immediately struck with the interpretation and application. You get two lines in and the Spirit just slams you with truth. You don't have to write a novel to please God. You might write down two words. You might write down no words because you have a baby you can't sit down and this whole process happens right in your head.

That's okay. Just give Him "what you can" each day, and trust that He will speak what your heart needs to hear.

I have always felt a special connection with this story because of the names of its characters. I cook in Martha's kitchen, *literally*. There is a colorful magnet on my refrigerator that says, "Martha's Kitchen," in bold, black letters. I am blessed to be able to raise my kids in the West Virginia farmhouse where my mother was raised, and where my dear grandmother, Martha, raised her own five children, as well as over one hundred foster children. The beautiful aroma of her life, which she poured out daily in service for Jesus, still permeates this house years after her homecoming to Heaven.

My grandmother Martha was probably the "Mary-est" person I ever met. The rocking chair where she met with Jesus every morning is still seated by our big, bay window, and serves as a constant reminder of what's really important.

If you were to give this passage a cold read, without any contextual knowledge of the Bible, you might walk away thinking, "God doesn't want me to do house chores." This would be followed by great rejoicing! "YES!!! The Bible is the **BEST BOOK EVER!** *Why didn't I pick this up sooner!?*"

You would be correct in assuming the Bible is the best book ever, but we know from the rest of Scripture that serving others is a good and Godly thing to do. Selflessly serving other people and showing hospitality are some of our primary means of showing the world the reality of Christ. So, the question becomes, *what did Martha get wrong*?

We get a clue with our key words, "anxious," "worried," and "distracted."

Martha was so obsessed with preparing the perfect meal for Jesus that she began to panic in an unhealthy way. I can just imagine her angry stomps around the kitchen. Maybe she's slamming doors and pots loud enough for Mary to hear in the other room. I can feel her fury building as she fumes under her breath, "I can't believe she's left me here to do this all by myself!" Finally, Martha can stand it no longer. Assured of her righteous position, she calls in Jesus to support her just cause and scold her wayward sister.

Perhaps if Mary had been brushing off her work to do something like binge *Netflix* or play Instagram reels, Martha may have had a valid reason to be upset. Maybe if their Guest hadn't been the Messiah, Martha could have been justified in her anger.

However, Mary wasn't binging Netflix and this was no ordinary Visitor. How many people can say that they had the chance to host the Son of God for dinner?

In this once-in-the-history-of-humanity scenario, Mary had chosen to set aside her chores for a time and sit down with Jesus. Martha wasn't wrong to want to show amazing hospitality to Jesus. She was wrong because of how she *valued* that act of service.

She was more worried about a table setting than the landscape of her heart.

She was more concerned about *feeding* Jesus than she was about being *fed by* Jesus.

Our serving becomes a distraction when it keeps us from doing the one thing that matters. God is more concerned about the condition of our hearts than the condition of our kitchen floors. So many of us make the daily choice to pursue good things, like clean floors, in the place of the "one thing that is necessary."

"It's not that Jesus didn't expect work to be done, meals to be made, and tables to be set; He simply called Martha to recognize opportunity for best in the midst of all that was good."(1)

Kitchen floors are going to get dirty again, the laundry is going to come unfolded again, that email inbox is going to get flooded again. The spiritual food Christ infuses into our souls when we choose to spend time with Him is the *one thing that cannot be taken away from us*. This doesn't mean we don't clean our floors. This simply means that if we have a choice between a clean floor, and a chance to sit and be with Jesus, *we make the choice to sit in the mess and be with Jesus.*

When I looked at this passage through the lens of the metanarrative of Scripture, I saw something I had never noticed before. In some ways, Mary and Martha serve as pictures of the Old and New covenant ways of relating to Christ.

We have Martha, diligently preparing a feast for Christ. Like any good Israeli housekeeper, she wants to impress her guests with this meal. Hospitality was one of the most important virtues in this culture. Martha's thinking, "After this over, I want to find a 5-star review on Yelp, given by the Son of God." Martha was working *for* God, but she was doing it *without God's help*, which only caused frustration and disappointment. The same thing happens to His servants today when we try to work for Him without Him.

Then we have Mary, and she doesn't seem to be at all worried about impressing Christ. She's not trying to "accomplish" anything. She knows what she has to give on her own is not enough, so she's not trying to feed Jesus, *she's letting Jesus feed her*. She knows that the opportunity to learn from Christ is more valuable than any 5-star review, and that His teaching will empower her for *real, impactful* service.

When we look at Martha and Mary, we see the shift from Law to Grace.

Law vs. Grace

Martha	Mary
TRYING TO IMPRESS GOD	THE JOY OF KNOWING HIM
TRYING TO IMPRESS OTHERS	FREED FROM OTHER'S OPINIONS
FINDING SIGNIFICANCE IN HER OWN ACCOMPLISHMENTS	THE JOY OF LIVING TO HONOR GOD.
SERVING GOD AS OUR DUTY	ENJOYING CHRIST AS OUR HEART'S GREATEST TREASURE

Maybe some of us are still living "trapped in the kitchen." We have received the grace of Christ, but we're still living to impress Him, rather than being *empowered by Him*.

This brings me back to Philippians 3, where Paul laments over the time he wasted attempting to impress God and impress men with his man-made righteousness (v. 8-9). He said all of his accolades were garbage compared to the joy of knowing Jesus. Paul found true joy for the first time when he threw his trophies in the trash and "let the dinner burn."

When we allow ourselves to pause from our "doing" and concentrate on our "becoming" by spending time in the Word, we will be better equipped to go back "to the kitchen" and serve others in a way that makes an eternal difference.

God doesn't call us to pause our work permanently. God empowered work is *good work*. He saved us by grace for "good works which He has prepared in advance for us to do" (Ephesians 2:10). We won't be able to accomplish these pre-ordained tasks if we aren't continually feeding ourselves with the Living Word. 2 Timothy 3:16-17 says, "All Scripture is God-breathed and is useful for teaching, rebuking, correcting, and training in righteousness so that the servant of God may be thoroughly equipped for every good work."

When we pause from our productivity to feast on Scripture, we will actually become *more* productive.

"All work, no matter how needed and useful, becomes anxious toiling if not fueled by our most needed sustenance: rest in the Lord."(2)

I find the strangest thing happens when I take time out to reorient myself in God's presence. When I seek Him first, the other duties in my life — like the 472 pairs of unmatched socks in my bedroom, the 200 tiny plastic figurines that have been dumped into the middle of the living room floor, the crumbs on the couch that seem to magically reappear the instant I turn around — somehow transform from tedious chores into opportunities.

I'm actually able to *thank* Him for this means of serving my family, and able to recognize that when I serve others, *I am actually serving Christ*. Tasks that seemed meaningless now have a clear and eternal purpose. It's only when I am steeped in the love of God, that I'm able to love others well. **When I have tasted and seen that He is good, I can savor Him in the serving.**

If we never stop to sample the Good Portion, we'll live like Martha — hungry, angry, and blustering around life feeling sorry for ourselves.

If we learn to be Mary's, and make feeding ourselves a priority, we can cook for others with a smile on our face and a skip in our step.

This brings us to the final part of Inductive study, the "Application."
How should this change the way I live?
Since we can only truly see ourselves through the lens of who God is, the first step in our application should be to ask, "What does this passage teach me about God?"(3)
I rephrased it a little differently in our template, but the intent is the same.

"HOW IS JESUS MORE LOVELY TO ME AFTER READING THIS PASSAGE?"

I can think of a hundred ways Christ is more lovely to me after soaking in this Scripture, but perhaps most prominently, I am reminded that He is the *God who sees*. Keeping up a home can be an extremely lonely and life-draining affair. How kind of God to remind me that I am never really alone. How kind of Him to invite me to rest in the midst of my straining.

I really want you to answer this question on your own. Take some time to admire Jesus in all of His grace-giving glory. Feel the love in His eyes as He invites you into His inner circle, and beckons you to sit at His feet.

Sit and savor.

To apply what we've learned, Wilkin suggests we ask,
"How does this aspect of God's character change my view of self?"
"What should I do in response?"(4)

Tim Keller has 5 questions which I believe are beneficial in letting Scripture reach in and rearrange our lives.(5)
Based on the truth revealed in this passage...
1) How can I praise Him?
2) How can I confess my sins on the basis of this text?
3) If this is really true, what wrong behavior, what harmful emotions or false attitudes result when I forget this? Every problem is because you have forgotten something. What problems are you facing?
4) What should I be aspiring to on the basis of this text?
5) Why is God telling me this today?

PART Prayer

P. PRAISE: GLORIFY GOD FOR WHO HE IS AND WHAT HE HAS DONE

A. ADMIT: CONFESS TO GOD WHERE YOU HAVE FALLEN SHORT

R. REQUEST: ASK GOD TO FORGIVE YOUR SIN AND TO MEET YOUR NEEDS

T. THANK: GIVE THANKS TO GOD FOR WHO HE IS AND WHAT HE HAS DONE

Perhaps the most crucial piece of this entire process is the part we don't write down. *It's the part we live.* In between the "Application" and the "Reflection" sections is the place where the romance takes shape, and we work "out" what God is working "in" us (Phil 2:12-13). It's where we "abide."

In our "Intimacy Is Ignited Through Obedience" portion, we discussed the importance of putting the things we have learned into practice. James says a man who hears the words of God but fails to act on them is, "Like a man who looks intently at his natural face in a mirror. For he looks at himself and goes away and at once forgets what he looks like" (James 1:23-24).

We are a naturally forgetful people, and now, a constantly distracted people. To remember will require a pre-planned strategy.

Jesus lays out the battle plan for successful spiritual growth in John 15, where He tells the disciples that they must learn to "abide" in Him if they want to be effective for His kingdom.
Before writing this book, I had never noticed the correlation Christ makes between abiding in Him and His words abiding in us. In verses 4-5, Christ explains the conditions for fruitfulness. "Abide in Me, and I in you…whoever abides in Me and I in him, he it is that bears much fruit, for apart from me, you can do nothing."

In verse 7, He repeats this admonition with slightly different wording. "Instead of saying, 'If you abide in Me, and I in you,' Jesus says, 'If you abide in me and my words abide in you.' I think the point of this change is to let us see practically how we let Jesus abide in us, namely, by letting His Word abide in us." (7) It's helpful for me to picture my heart as a garden when I think about abiding. In Matthew 13, Christ compares the human heart to different types of soil. When God "sows" the Truth of the Gospel into our lives, it either takes root and produces fruit, or it fails to blossom into maturity.

If you are in Christ, your heart is "good" soil. Christ has taken root in your soul. In James 1:21, we are commanded to, "receive with meekness the implanted word."

This command is fascinating to me! The word has been "implanted" in us, *past* tense. But we are still commanded to "receive" it on an ongoing, *present tense*, basis. It's as if the Word already in us is fed and nourished by the Word we continually intake. When we choose to meditate on Truth throughout the day, the sunshine of our attention causes the garden of our hearts to flourish and thrive. When we are continuously distracted, by bad or even "good" things, our gardens begin to wither. Our insides start to look like dry, cracked earth. The Word is still there, waiting to bloom into something beautiful, but we just don't give it a chance to grow. The Message puts it this way, "So throw away all spoiled virtue and cancerous evil in the garbage, let our gardener, God, landscape you with the Word, making a salvation-garden of your life" (James 1:21 MSG).

I want my heart to be a living Eden, a place where Christ and I can walk in sweet fellowship, like an inner oasis where I can find refuge from the world.

"SO THROW AWAY ALL SPOILED VIRTUE AND CANCEROUS EVIL IN THE GARBAGE, LET OUR GARDENER, GOD, LANDSCAPE YOU WITH THE WORD, MAKING A SALVATION-GARDEN OF YOUR LIFE."

−James 1:21 MSG

PRACTICAL STRATEGIES WE CAN USE TO HELP CULTIVATE THE GARDEN OF OUR HEARTS

BATTLE PLAN #1- PHYSICAL REMINDERS

In Deuteronomy, God gives the Israelites instructions for remembering His commands. "Fix these words of mine in your hearts and minds; tie them as symbols on your hands and bind them on your foreheads. Teach them to your children, talking about them when you sit at home and when you walk along the road, when you lie down and when you get up. Write them on the doorframes of your houses and on your gates" (Deuteronomy 11:18-20).

He wants them to "fix" His words in their hearts by *physically* fixing them in places they will encounter all day, every day. Back then, they wrote the Word on their doorposts and their gates. We can still do this today, but we can also place His Word on our bathroom mirrors, in our cars, as the wallpaper on our phones, and as the pictures we place on our mantle. We are in a constant battle for our eyes. Screens are everywhere, crying out for our attention. Why not put His Word everywhere, and redirect our thoughts from Hulu to the heavenlies?

In the back of this book, we have included blank Scripture memory cards. We want you to cut them out and go crazy sticking them everywhere. I purchased a handful of adorable place card holders that look like miniature potted plants. Instead of stuffing them with seating arrangements, I stuffed them with Scripture. If you don't want to cut things out, get some index cards. Do what works for you! I have a friend who writes all over her stainless steel appliances with neon, dry erase markers. *Get creative!*

BATTLE PLAN #2 — MEMORIZATION

Memorization has become a lost art in the age of computers. We don't feel the necessity of storing anything in our minds since we have all the answers stored on *Google*. I sometimes feel as if I carry my brain around in my pocket. I use this as an excuse to forgo memorizing Scripture, since I can simply look up the reference to any verse I want with a few flicks of my fingers.

God did not only command the Israelites to merely affix the Word to their houses, but to their hearts and to their souls (Deuteronomy 6:18). I have recently been convicted about the need for memorization as I have been reading through the autobiography of Brother Yun(8), a Chinese Christian who was imprisoned and brutally tortured for his faith. Yun began memorizing large portions of Scripture as a teenager, including the entire book of Matthew. This practice proved invaluable during his time in jail when he did not have access to a Bible. He had memorized such massive sections of Scripture that he was able to faithfully teach the Bible to his fellow prisoners without having a physical copy of the Word to reference.

Well, Brooke, you may be saying, "I don't plan on being imprisoned in a communist hard-labor camp anytime soon." This may be true, but it is best not to wait until you are in the midst of a crisis or a difficult situation before you reach for Scripture.

BLESSED IS THE MAN WHO WALKS NOT IN THE COUNSEL OF THE WICKED NOR STANDS IN THE WAY OF SINNERS, NOR SITS IN THE SEAT OF SCOFFERS; BUT HIS DELIGHT IS IN THE LAW[B] OF THE LORD, AND ON HIS LAW HE MEDITATES DAY AND NIGHT. HE IS LIKE A TREE PLANTED BY STREAMS OF WATER THAT YIELDS ITS FRUIT IN ITS SEASON AND ITS LEAF DOES NOT WITHER. IN ALL THAT HE DOES, HE PROSPERS.

Psalm 1:1-3

John Piper suggests that we create a "reservoir" of Scripture in our minds that we can pull from when we walk through the wilderness.(9)

Ruth Chou Simons says that when her thoughts begin to spiral into anxiety, she often reaches for, "the low-hanging fruit of my own muddled thoughts and....I come up short of what I truly need."(10) When we fill our minds with Scripture, we are able to reach for and find just the right encouragement we need, when we need it. We don't have time to reach for our phones to do research when all the co-workers are gossiping around the lunch table and we're invited to join in, when we are tempted to shout at the ref at a child's ball game, when our crying kid rushes into our arms, needing advice. Simons says we don't just need to know how to "find" something in God's Word, we need to own truth for ourselves through memorization.

"Can you imagine it? Rather than scrambling and digging around to find the truth about who you are and what really matters — trying to weed out the clutter and to get to the good — imagine accessing the truth immediately because, more than merely available, it is yours."(11)
I'm sure we've all encountered the sweetness of a mature Christian who is so saturated with Scripture, it seems to ooze from their being, flavoring their every conversation with Christ. I love being around these sorts of people, and want to *become* this sort of person.

Simons says that if our hearts were like houses, the rooms of such a person's heart would be, "so taken over by truth that he is unable to entertain sin."(12) This led me to think of "walking the halls" of my own heart, and wishing they'd be wallpapered with Scripture. Throughout this book, I have scattered pages completely covered in the Word. As I crafted each page, I imagined I was plastering these words onto the walls of my heart.

I have left the next two pages blank for you to start thinking about what verses you would like to use to "wallpaper" your heart. What truths do you want in your "reservoir" so you can reach for them at anytime?

One day, I would love to fit the description that Charles Spurgeon gave to author John Bunyan, "Why this man is a living Bible! Prick him anywhere —his blood is Bibline, the very essence of the Bible flows from him."(13)

Let's journey together toward becoming "living Bibles." I want my reservoir to be so full that I can overflow with His Truth into the lives of others!

THE WALLS OF ˗˗˗˗˗˗˗˗˗˗˗˗ HEART

THE WALLS OF _____ HEART

WOOOOOOOOOOOOOOOOOOOOOOOOOOOOOOOOOOOOOOOOOOOOOOOOOOOOOOOOOOOOOOOO!

(I'm out of breath!)

We have reached the final section in our journals -- the "Reflection!"

See, look at you! I *knew* you could do it!

After our time of abiding and living out the Word, we should take some time to reflect on what we have learned. This section helps keep us accountable to not leave the Word on our bed stand or inside our phone screens.

How do you know Jesus more now than you did at the beginning of the day?

How did you encounter Him today?

How are you a different person than you were before you discovered this passage of Scripture?

The real evidence will be built into your heart, the one thing in your life that no one can take from you.

WOOOOOOOOOOOOOOOOOOOOOOOOOOOOOOOOOOOOOOOOOOOOOOOOOOOOOOOOOOOOOOOOOOOOOOOOOOOOOOOOOOOOOOOOOOOOOOOOOOOOOOOOOOOO!

(I just had to do it one more time!)

Well, Sisters, it looks like our journey together has come to an end. Before I set you loose to do your own Bible digging, there is one last thought I want to leave with you.

Sometimes, after we've journeyed long with Jesus, we may come to believe we've got a handle on this whole Christianity thing, and begin to assume we know pretty much all there is to know. We may not voice this out loud, but deep down, we may think we have explored the depths of Christ's heart. This is a dangerous mindset and indicates we have a view of God that's far too small.

Ephesians 3:8 tells us that Christ's riches are "unsearchable." We are never going to "get" Him. If you find yourself stagnant in your walk with Christ, "Let me suggest that you consider the possibility that your current mental idea of Jesus is the tip of the iceberg."(14)

I will never forget my first day of theology class in college. The professor drew an iceberg on the board, leaving only its bright white peak visible above the surface of the waters. This image represents the pursuit of the knowledge of God. All we could learn about Christ in this lifetime, or in a hundred lifetimes, is merely the "tip of the iceberg." And it's not just any iceberg-- it's an *infinite* iceberg that goes on forever and only gets wider and wider as it grows toward the depths of an infinite sea. If we feel bored, maybe we just need to "trade in our snorkel and face mask for scuba gear that takes us down into depths we've never peered into before." (15)

Another illustration that has stuck with me since childhood is C.S. Lewis's description of Heaven found in, "The Last Battle." The main characters discover they have died on earth and are now in the Narnian version of the afterlife. This revelation is not met with sadness but greeted with great joy. The land is glorious and they find no matter how far they travel, there is only more beauty left to discover. They encourage one another to press on into paradise with the cry, "Come further up, come further in!"(16)

Sisters, we will forever and always be going, "Further up and further in" into the wonders of Jesus. **We are always *just beginning* to know Him.**
Until we meet on the other side, "Further up and further in!" my friends,
"Further up and further in..."

If you fill up this journal, and find you enjoy this style of Bible study, you can continue to do it in your own notebook, or purchase "The Good Portion Journal." This book contains only blank journal pages so you can continue in your journey. Don't forget to check out the memory verse cards, resource page, and study questions at the back of this book!

Bible Study Journal Pages

Scripture:

Date: / /

POUR IT OUT

OBSERVATION/INTERPRETATION

HOW IS JESUS MORE LOVELY TO ME?

APPLICATION

PRAYER

Abide

REFLECTION

Scripture: Date: / /

POUR IT OUT

OBSERVATION/INTERPRETATION

HOW IS JESUS MORE LOVELY TO ME?

APPLICATION

PRAYER

Abide

REFLECTION

Scripture: Date: / /

POUR IT OUT

OBSERVATION/INTERPRETATION

HOW IS JESUS MORE LOVELY TO ME?

APPLICATION

PRAYER

Abide

REFLECTION

Scripture: Date: / /

POUR IT OUT

OBSERVATION/INTERPRETATION

HOW IS JESUS MORE LOVELY TO ME?

APPLICATION

PRAYER

Abide

REFLECTION

Scripture:

Date: / /

POUR IT OUT

OBSERVATION/INTERPRETATION

HOW IS JESUS MORE LOVELY TO ME?

APPLICATION

PRAYER

~ Abide ~

REFLECTION

Scripture:

Date: / /

POUR IT OUT

OBSERVATION/INTERPRETATION

HOW IS JESUS MORE LOVELY TO ME?

APPLICATION

PRAYER

~ Abide ~

REFLECTION

Scripture: Date: / /

POUR IT OUT

OBSERVATION/INTERPRETATION

HOW IS JESUS MORE LOVELY TO ME?

APPLICATION

PRAYER

~ Abide ~

REFLECTION

Scripture: Date: / /

POUR IT OUT

OBSERVATION/INTERPRETATION

HOW IS JESUS MORE LOVELY TO ME?

APPLICATION

PRAYER

Abide

REFLECTION

Scripture: Date: / /

POUR IT OUT

OBSERVATION/INTERPRETATION

HOW IS JESUS MORE LOVELY TO ME?

APPLICATION

PRAYER

~ Abide ~

REFLECTION

Scripture: Date: / /

POUR IT OUT

OBSERVATION/INTERPRETATION

HOW IS JESUS MORE LOVELY TO ME?

APPLICATION

PRAYER

Abide

REFLECTION

Scripture: Date: / /

POUR IT OUT

OBSERVATION/INTERPRETATION

HOW IS JESUS MORE LOVELY TO ME?

APPLICATION

PRAYER

Abide

REFLECTION

Scripture: Date: / /

POUR IT OUT

OBSERVATION/INTERPRETATION

HOW IS JESUS MORE LOVELY TO ME?

APPLICATION

PRAYER

Abide

REFLECTION

Scripture: _____ Date: __/__/__

POUR IT OUT

OBSERVATION/INTERPRETATION

HOW IS JESUS MORE LOVELY TO ME?

APPLICATION

PRAYER

Abide

REFLECTION

Scripture: Date: / /

POUR IT OUT

OBSERVATION/INTERPRETATION

HOW IS JESUS MORE LOVELY TO ME?

APPLICATION

PRAYER

Abide

REFLECTION

Scripture:

Date: / /

POUR IT OUT

OBSERVATION/INTERPRETATION

HOW IS JESUS MORE LOVELY TO ME?

APPLICATION

PRAYER

~ Abide ~

REFLECTION

Scripture: Date: / /

POUR IT OUT

OBSERVATION/INTERPRETATION

HOW IS JESUS MORE LOVELY TO ME?

APPLICATION

PRAYER

~ Abide ~

REFLECTION

Scripture: Date: / /

POUR IT OUT

OBSERVATION/INTERPRETATION

HOW IS JESUS MORE LOVELY TO ME?

APPLICATION

PRAYER

Abide

REFLECTION

Scripture: Date: / /

POUR IT OUT

OBSERVATION/INTERPRETATION

HOW IS JESUS MORE LOVELY TO ME?

APPLICATION

PRAYER

Abide

REFLECTION

Scripture: Date: / /

POUR IT OUT

OBSERVATION/INTERPRETATION

HOW IS JESUS MORE LOVELY TO ME?

APPLICATION

PRAYER

— Abide —

REFLECTION

Scripture: Date: / /

POUR IT OUT

OBSERVATION/INTERPRETATION

HOW IS JESUS MORE LOVELY TO ME?

APPLICATION

PRAYER

~ Abide ~

REFLECTION

Scripture: Date: / /

POUR IT OUT

OBSERVATION/INTERPRETATION

HOW IS JESUS MORE LOVELY TO ME?

APPLICATION

PRAYER

Abide

REFLECTION

Scripture: Date: / /

POUR IT OUT

OBSERVATION/INTERPRETATION

HOW IS JESUS MORE LOVELY TO ME?

APPLICATION

PRAYER

Abide

REFLECTION

Scripture: Date: / /

POUR IT OUT

OBSERVATION/INTERPRETATION

HOW IS JESUS MORE LOVELY TO ME?

APPLICATION

PRAYER

Abide

REFLECTION

Scripture:

Date: / /

POUR IT OUT

OBSERVATION/INTERPRETATION

HOW IS JESUS MORE LOVELY TO ME?

APPLICATION

PRAYER

Abide

REFLECTION

Scripture: Date: / /

POUR IT OUT

OBSERVATION/INTERPRETATION

HOW IS JESUS MORE LOVELY TO ME?

APPLICATION

PRAYER

Abide

REFLECTION

Scripture: Date: / /

POUR IT OUT

OBSERVATION/INTERPRETATION

HOW IS JESUS MORE LOVELY TO ME?

APPLICATION

PRAYER

Abide

REFLECTION

Scripture: Date: / /

POUR IT OUT

OBSERVATION/INTERPRETATION

HOW IS JESUS MORE LOVELY TO ME?

APPLICATION

PRAYER

Abide

REFLECTION

Scripture:

Date: / /

POUR IT OUT

OBSERVATION/INTERPRETATION

HOW IS JESUS MORE LOVELY TO ME?

APPLICATION

PRAYER

Abide

REFLECTION

Scripture: Date: / /

POUR IT OUT

OBSERVATION/INTERPRETATION

HOW IS JESUS MORE LOVELY TO ME?

APPLICATION

PRAYER

~ Abide ~

REFLECTION

Scripture: Date: / /

POUR IT OUT

OBSERVATION/INTERPRETATION

HOW IS JESUS MORE LOVELY TO ME?

APPLICATION

PRAYER

~ Abide ~

REFLECTION

 Questions

FOR PERSONAL REFLECTION

&

GROUP DISCUSSION

These questions can be used purely for personal devotional use or discussed in a group setting. If you want to use this book as a weekly Bible study, you might find it helpful to break up the chapters in the following way:

WEEK 1 - INTRODUCTION & EVERY WOMAN'S BATTLE

WEEK 2 - SEE THE BIGGER STORY & INVITATION TO INTIMACY

WEEK 3 - INTIMACY BEGINS WITH INFORMATION, INTIMACY REQUIRES INTENTIONALITY, & INTIMACY IS IGNITED THROUGH OBEDIENCE

WEEK 4 - ROMANCING THE MIND

WEEK 5 - WHY PROCESS MATTERS & THE OBSERVATION PORTION OF INDUCTIVE STUDY

WEEK 6 - THE INTERPRETATION, APPLICATION, PRAYER, ABIDE, & REFLECTION PORTIONS OF INDUCTIVE STUDY

Introduction

HOW OFTEN DO YOU FEED YOURSELF ON THE NOURISHMENT OF THE WORD?

WHEN YOU SKIP A BIBLE STUDY, DO YOU NOTICE A DIFFERENCE?

WHY DO YOU THINK IT'S SO MUCH EASIER TO SKIP OUR TIME IN THE WORD THAN IT IS TO SKIP A MEAL?

THINK OF ONE TIME WHEN SCRIPTURE HELPED YOU "SEE" CLEARLY IN A DIFFICULT SITUATION.

HOW DOES THE IDEA OF "EATING" SCRIPTURE CHANGE YOUR PERSPECTIVE ON STUDYING SCRIPTURE?

HOW WOULD YOU CATEGORIZE YOURSELF-
A) WANT TO STUDY THE WORD BUT DON'T KNOW HOW/ARE INTIMIDATED
B) WANT TO STUDY THE WORD BUT FEEL YOU DON'T HAVE TIME
C) STUDY THE WORD ON A REGULAR BASIS BUT WANT TO GET MORE FROM THE EXPERIENCE

Every Woman's Battle

- HOW DO YOU RELATE TO THE WOMAN IN THIS SCENARIO?

- HAVE YOU EVER FELT CONFUSED OR OVERWHELMED BY A PASSAGE OF SCRIPTURE?

- IN CHRIST'S TIME, THE PHRASE, "TO SIT AT HIS FEET," INDICATED THAT MARY WAS SITTING AND LEARNING ALONGSIDE CHRIST'S DISCIPLES. IN THIS CULTURE, WOMEN WERE DENIED ACCESS TO HIGHER EDUCATION. HOW DOES IT MAKE YOU FEEL TO KNOW THAT JESUS BROKE THE MOLD AND INVITED WOMEN TO COME AND LEARN FROM HIM?(1)

- WHAT WOULD IT LOOK LIKE FOR YOU TO GIVE HIM "WHAT YOU CAN" TODAY?

See The Bigger Story

- HAVE YOU EVER THOUGHT OF THE BIBLE AS ONE BIG STORY BEFORE?

- WHEN YOU GO TO SCRIPTURE, IS YOUR FIRST INSTINCT TO LOOK FOR YOURSELF OR TO LOOK FOR JESUS?

- DO YOU HAVE ANY FAVORITE "STRANDS OF PEARLS"? DO SOME RESEARCH ON YOUR OWN AND SEE IF YOU CAN "STRING THE PEARLS" OF MARRIAGE FOUND THROUGHOUT THE BIBLE.

Invitation To Intimacy

-Have you ever thought of yourself as the bride of Christ? Does this increase your excitement for eternity?

-How does this change the way you view your sin and sanctification?

-Get honest with God. Are you in union with Him? Have you ever personally accepted His gift of eternal life and become His bride? If not, *change that today!*

-If you are in union with Christ, evaluate the state of your "communion." Could you use a dash of "blushing-bride" excitement?

Intimacy Begins With Information

- HAVE YOU EVER BEEN TEMPTED TO BELIEVE THAT CHRISTIANITY WAS ABOUT A LIST OF RULES TO FOLLOW OR FACTS TO MEMORIZE? WHO DO YOU KNOW WHO THINKS THIS WAY?

- HAS YOUR APPROACH TO SPIRITUAL GROWTH BEEN TO "SKIP THE HEAD AND GO STRAIGHT FOR THE HEART"?

- MEDITATE ON THE STATEMENT, "THE HEART CANNOT LOVE WHAT THE MIND DOES NOT KNOW." WHAT DO YOU KNOW ABOUT GOD THAT HAS MADE YOU FALL IN LOVE WITH HIM?

Intimacy Requires Intentionality

-How have you had to be intentional in your relationships with other people? How have you seen a breakdown in your relationships when you're not intentional in spending real time with them?

-Have you ever viewed your time in the Word as a meeting with a real, living God? How does this make you feel?

-Do you approach your time with the Lord like I approached my nightly call with Kyle? Does your heart thrill and yearn to be alone with Him?

-Have you woken up to a cold heart instead of a cold house? What can you do to "stoke the fire" today?

Intimacy Is Ignited Through Obedience

-HAVE YOU EVER FELT THE CALL TO OBEY GOD WAS CONFUSING OR DEMANDING? HOW HAS THIS CHAPTER CHANGED YOUR PERSPECTIVE?

-HAVE YOU EVER EXPERIENCED "CHRIST'S HEART BEATING THROUGH YOUR OWN"? WHEN?

-WHAT ARE SOME AREAS IN YOUR LIFE WHERE YOU'VE BEEN HOLDING ONTO SIN BECAUSE YOU ARE AFRAID GOD WON'T BE ABLE TO SATISFY YOU?

-DO YOU TEND TO ACT OUT OF YOUR FEELINGS? IN WHAT WAYS DO YOU NEED CHRIST TO CHANGE YOUR MIND SO YOU CAN ACT AND FEEL DIFFERENTLY?

-HAVE YOU LOST YOUR "FIRST LOVE"? LIST SOME OF THE THINGS YOU REMEMBER DOING WHEN YOU FIRST MET JESUS. KEEP DOING THEM OR START DOING THEM AGAIN!

Romancing the Mind

-WHAT SORTS OF SOCIAL MEDIA ABSORB THE MOST OF YOUR MIND AND YOUR TIME? HAVE YOU BEEN UTILIZING THEM IN HEALTHY WAYS, OR DO YOU FEEL THE PULL OF ADDICTION?

-DO YOU FIND YOURSELF USING YOUR PHONE AS A WAY TO EMOTIONALLY ESCAPE FROM DIFFICULT SITUATIONS? WHAT IS ONE "HARD THING" YOU HAVE BEEN PUTTING OFF THAT YOU CAN FACE TODAY?

-WHAT TIMES OF DAY ARE YOU MOST VULNERABLE TO BINGE ON YOUR PHONE? WHAT ARE SOME HEALTHY REPLACEMENT ACTIVITIES YOU CAN DO INSTEAD?

-PERFORM AN EXPERIMENT -- TODAY, TRY TO CATCH YOURSELF WHEN YOU REACH UNCONSCIOUSLY FOR YOUR PHONE. COUNT HOW OFTEN IT HAPPENS AND TRY CUTTING THE NUMBER DOWN THE NEXT DAY. TO HELP, REARRANGE THE ICONS ON YOUR PHONE. EVEN BETTER -- DELETE YOUR APPS ALTOGETHER SO YOU ARE FORCED TO USE YOUR WEB BROWSER. DOWNLOAD THE "YOUVERSION" APP OR THE "FIRST 5" APP AS REPLACEMENTS.

-REPLACE THE WALLPAPER ON YOUR PHONE WITH SCRIPTURE.

Why Process Matters

-HAD YOU EVER THOUGHT OF CULTIVATING A PROPER STUDY PROCESS AS A MEANS OF LOVING GOD?

-HAVE YOU EVER ENGAGED IN ANY OF THESE UNHEALTHY METHODS OF STUDYING SCRIPTURE? IF SO, WHICH ONES?

-PRAY AND ASK GOD TO HELP YOU TO NOT BE INTIMIDATED, BUT EXCITED ABOUT WORKING WITH THE HOLY SPIRIT IN THE STUDY OF HIS WORD.

Observation

-CHOOSE YOUR OWN PORTION OF SCRIPTURE TO STUDY.
USE THE CHARTS ON PAGES 81, 83-84, AND 86 TO HELP ASK THE "W" QUESTIONS FOR BOTH THE BOOK OF THE BIBLE AND THE CHOSEN TEXT.

-USE THE CHART ON PAGE 87 TO HELP YOU LOCATE ANY KEY WORDS AND PHRASES.

Interpretation

-ASK THE "WHY" AND THE "HOW" QUESTIONS.

WHY DOES THIS MATTER?

HOW WOULD THE ORIGINAL AUDIENCE HAVE UNDERSTOOD THIS?

Application

-HOW SHOULD THIS CHANGE THE WAY YOU LIVE?

HOW IS JESUS MORE LOVELY TO YOU AFTER READING THIS STORY?

HOW SHOULD THIS ALTER THE WAY YOU THINK AND THE WAY YOU ACT?

Prayer

- Take some time to get alone with God and thank Him for the gift of His word. Ask Him to awaken your hunger to know Him. Make a "battle plan" for how you will make "eating your portion" a regular habit.

- Pick a verse or two you want to memorize and fill out scripture memory cards. Hang them in a place where you'll see them every day.

Recommended Resources

MORE TIPS ON PERSONAL BIBLE STUDY:

Kay Arthur, David Arthur, and Pete De Lacey, *The New How to Study Your Bible* (Eugene, Oregon: Harvest House, 2010)

Gordon D. Fee and Douglas Stuart, *How To Read The Bible Book For All Its Worth* (Grand Rapids: Zondervan Academic, 2014)

Jen Wilkin, *Women Of The Word: How To Study The Bible With Both Our Hearts and Our Minds*, Second Edition (Wheaton: Crossway, 2014)

Robert H. Stein. *A Basic Guide To Interpreting The Bible: Playing By The Rules*, Second Edition(Grand Rapids: Baker Academic, 2011)

METANARRATIVE/CULTURAL & HISTORICAL CONTEXT:

Tara Leigh Coble, *The Bible Recap: A One Year Guide To Reading The Bible* (Minneapolis: Bethany House, 2020)
Also available as a free podcast on major podcast platforms.

Gordon D. Fee and Douglas Stuart, *How To Read The Bible Book By Book: A Guided Tour* (Grand Rapids: Zondervan Academic, 2014)

Kay Arthur, *Discover The Bible For Yourself*, (Eugene, Oregon: Harvest House, 2000).

Kristi McClelland, Pearls With Kristi McLelland, Accessmore.com, podcast audio, January 2022, Apple Podcasts

Kenneth Bailey, *Jesus Through Middle Eastern Eyes*, (Eugene, Oregon: Harvest House, 2000).

FREE ONLINE BIBLE STUDY TOOLS

Blue Letter Bible. Available at www.blueletterbible.org

BibleGateway. Available at www.biblegateway.org

Biblehub. Available at www.biblehub.org

NOTES

INTRODUCTION

1. Lifeway Reseach, How Often Do You Read The Bible: Among Protestant Churchgoers (July 2, 2019), distributed by Lifeway Research, https://research.lifeway.com/2019/07/02/few-protestant-churchgoers-read-the-bible-daily/
2. McLelland, Kristi. Stringing The Biblical Pearls, Pearls With Kristi McLelland, podcast audio, January 31, 2022.
3. McLelland, Kristi. Stringing The Biblical Pearls

EVERY WOMAN'S BATTLE

1. Traci Beck Arnwine and Heather F., "THIS HIT ME HARD," Facebook, January, 16, 2021, https://www.facebook.com/traci.beckarnwine/posts/10219775115800421.
2. Traci Beck Arnwine and Heather F., "THIS HIT ME HARD."
3. Luke 10:42, ESV

SEE THE BIGGER STORY

1. Eugene Peterson, *Eat This Book: A Conversation In The Art of Spiritual Reading* (Grand Rapids: Eerdmans, 2009) E-book.
2. Sally Loyd Jones, *The Jesus Storybook Bible: Every Story Whispers His Name* (Nashville: Zonderkidz, 2009).
3. The Christy Wright Show, "How To Better Understand Who God Is With Kristi McLelland," YouTube Video, 26:18, October 19, 2020, https://www.youtube.com/watchv=vhDmMQ2vzYQ.
4. The Christy Wright Show, "How To Better Understand Who God Is With Kristi McLelland."
5. The Christy Wright Show, "How To Better Understand Who God Is With Kristi McLelland."
6. Gordon D. Fee and Douglas Stuart, *How To Read The Bible Book By Book* (Grand Rapids: Zondervan, 2002), E-book, 28.
7. Gordon D. Fee and Douglas Stuart, *How To Read The Bible Book By Book*, 22.
8. Gordon D. Fee and Douglas Stuart, *How To Read The Bible Book By Book*, 27.

9. Trillia J. Newbell, *God's Very Good Idea Storybook: A True Story of God's Delightfully Different Family* (Epsom, Surrey: The Good Book Company, 2017)

10. McLelland, Kristi. Stringing The Biblical Pearls.

11. John Piper, "The Bible will not give its riches to those who will not dig," SermonQuotes, January 18, 2018, https://sermonquotes.com/bible/14061-the-bible-will-not-give-its-riches-to-those-who-will-not-dig-john-piper.html.

INVITATION TO INTIMACY

1. Sinclair Ferguson, *The Trinitarian Devotion of John Owen* (Lake Mary, FL : Reformation Trust, 2014), 64, as quoted in Rankin Wilbourne, *Union With Christ: The Way To Know And Enjoy God* (Colorado Springs: David C. Cook, 2016), 110.

2. Rankin Wilbourne, *Union With Christ: The Way To Know And Enjoy God* (Colorado Springs: David C. Cook, 2016), 11.

3. John Owen, Edited by Kelly M. Kapic and Justin Taylor, *Communion With The Triune God* (Wheaton: Crossway Books, 2007) E-book, 26.

4. Spurgeon, Charles Haddon. "The Fourfold Treasure." Metropolitan Tabernacle Pulpit, Volume 17, April 26, 1871.

INTIMACY BEGINS WITH INFORMATION

1. Jen Wilkin, *Women Of The Word: How To Study The Bible With Both Our Hearts and Our Minds*, Second Edition (Wheaton: Crossway, 2014). E-book, 29.

2. Wilkin, *Women Of The Word: How To Study The Bible With Both Our Hearts And Our Minds*, 45.

INTIMACY REQUIRES INTENTIONALITY

1. John Piper, "If My Words Abide In You," Desiring God, January 3, 1993, Accessed March 1, 2022, https://www.desiringgod.org/messages/if-my-words-abide-in-you.

2. The Christy Wright Show, "How To Better Understand Who God Is With Kristi McLelland."

INTIMACY IS IGNITED THROUGH OBEDIENCE

1. Chip Ingram, "Does Love Equal Obedience?" Living On The Edge, https://livingontheedge.org/2017/11/10/does-love-equal-obedience/.

2. Wilbourne, *Union With God: The Way To Know And Enjoy God*, 246.
3. John Piper, "United With Christ In Death And Life, Part One," Desiring God, Messages, September 24, 2000, Accessed April 4th 2022, https://www.desiringgod.org/messages/united-with-christ-in-death-and-life-part-1
4. Tony Evans, "Praying Through A Crisis-Sermon by Tony Evans," 27:40, March 20, 2022, https://www.youtube.com/watch?v=UN_HXqjCX2w.
5. John Piper, "What's The Origin Of Desiring God's Slogan," Desiring God, Ask Pastor John, Episode 1096, September 20,2017, Audio Transcript, https://www.desiringgod.org/interviews/whats-the-origin-of-desiring-gods-slogan
6. Wilbourne, *Union With God: The Way To Know And Enjoy God*, 119-120.
7. Jim Goforth (New Life Community Church),"How To Become More Loving: Building Better Relationships," Youtube Video, March 16, 2022, https://www.youtube.com/watch?v=KcU8QMbCGf8.
8. Jim Goforth (New Life Community Church),"How To Become More Loving: Building Better Relationships,
9. Manifest. 2018 "Reentry." NBC. Duration of Video, October 1, 2018, 41 minutes.

ROMANCING THE MIND

1. Marshall Segal, "The Blissful and Trivial Life: How Entertainment Deprives A Soul." Desiring God, February 27, 2022, https://www.desiringgod.org/articles/the-blissful-and-trivial-life
2. Marshall Segal, "The Blissful and Trivial Life: How Entertainment Deprives A Soul."
3. Bruce Goldman, "The Addictive Potential of Social Media, Explained," Scope 10k, Stanford Medicine, October 29, 2021, https://scopeblog.stanford.edu/2021/10/29/addictive-potential-of-social-media-explained/
4. Bruce Goldman, "The Addictive Potential of Social Media, Explained."
5. Trevor Haynes and Rebecca Clements, "Dopamine, Smartphones, and You: A Battle For Your Time," Harvard, Science In The News Blog, May 1, 2018, https://sitn.hms.harvard.edu/flash/2018/dopamine-smartphones-battle-time/
6. Michael Winnick, "Putting A Finger On Our Phone Obsession: Mobile Touches: A Study In How Humans Use Technology," dscout, People Nerds, https://dscout.com/people-nerds/mobile-touches
7. Bruce Goldman, "The Addictive Potential of Social Media, Explained."
8. Jamie Waters, "Constant Craving: How Digital Media Turned Us All Into Dopamine Addicts," The Guardian, Life and Style, August 22,2021 https://www.google.com/amp/s/amp.theguardian.com/global/2021/aug/22/how-digital-media-turned-us-all-into-dopamine-addicts-and-what-we-can-do-to-break-the-cycle

9. C.S. Lewis, *Mere Christianity: A revised and amplified edition, with a new introduction, of the three books Broadcast Talks, Christian Behaviour and Beyond Personality* (Harper Collins E-books, 2021), E-book, 63.

10. Tony Reinke, "Who Will Have Your Attention? Clinging To Christ In The Digital Age?" Sing! Global 2020 Conference, Desiring God, November 15, 2020, https://www.desiringgod.org/messages/who-will-have-your-attention.

11. Tony Reinke, "Who Will Have Your Attention? Clinging To Christ In The Digital Age?"

12. Tony Reinke, "Who Will Have Your Attention? Clinging To Christ In The Digital Age?"

13. Dane Ortlund, *Gentle And Lowly: The Heart Of Christ For Sinners and Sufferers* (Wheaton: Crossway, 2020) 99.

14. Sally Clarkson and Sarah Clarkson, *The Life-giving Home: Creating A Place of Belonging & Becoming*(Illinois: Tyndale Momentum, 2016) 61.

15. Sally Clarkson and Sarah Clarkson, *The Life-giving Home: Creating A Place of Belonging & Becoming*, 64.

16. Dr. Kim and Dr. Hil, "Neural Plasticity: 4 Steps to Change Your Brain & Habits," Authenticity Associates Coaching & Counseling, June 21, 2010,https://www.authenticityassociates.com/neural-plasticity-4-steps-to-change-your brain/#:~:text=Hiking%20trails%20are%20similar%20to,you%20strengthen%20your%20brain%20pathways.

WHY PROCESS MATTERS?

1. Lysa Terkheurst, *Trustworthy, A Study of 1 &2 Kings: Overcoming Our Greatest Struggles to Trust God* (Nashville: Lifeway Press, 2019), 78.

2. Randy Alcorn, "How The Holy Spirit Helps You Read The Word of God," Eternal Perspective Ministries, Biblestudytools.com, https://www.biblestudytools.com/bible-study/topical-studies/the-holy-spirit-the-word-of-god-and-you.html.

3. Alcorn, "How The Holy Spirit Helps Us Understand The Word of God."

4. Eugene Peterson, *Living The Message* (San Francisco: Harper Collins, 1996).

5. Wilkin, *Women Of The Word: How To Study The Bible With Both Our Hearts And Our Minds.*

6. Keller, Timothy. Father, Son and Holy Spirit, Timothy Keller Sermons By Gospel In Life, podcast audio, April 4, 2022.

7. Wilkin, *Women Of The Word: How To Study The Bible With Both Our Hearts And Our Minds.*

8. Lysa Terkheurst, *Trustworthy, A Study of 1 &2 Kings: Overcoming Our Greatest Struggles to Trust God* (Nashville: Lifeway Press, 2019), 78.

HOW TO STUDY THE BIBLE

1. Ruth Chou Simons, *Beholding and Becoming: The Art of Everyday Worship*(Oregon: Harvest House Publishers, 2020)203.
2. Ruth Chou Simons, *Beholding and Becoming: The Art of Everyday Worship*,203.
3. Jen Wilkin, *Women Of The Word: How To Study The Bible With Both Our Hearts and Our Minds*, 97.
4. Jen Wilkin, *Women Of The Word: How To Study The Bible With Both Our Hearts and Our Minds*, 97.
5. Tim Keller, "5 Questions God Dr. Tim Keller Asks Of A Biblical Passage," lifecoach4God, October 16, 2012, https://lifecoach4god.life/2012/10/16/5-questions-dr-tim-keller-asks-of-a-biblical-passage/, Accessed April 30, 2022.
6. Jen Wilkin, *Women Of The Word: How To Study The Bible With Both Our Hearts and Our Minds*. 101.
7. John Piper, "If My Words Abide In You," Desiring God, January 3, 1993, Accessed March 1, 2022, https://www.desiringgod.org/messages/if-my-words-abide-in-you.
8. Brother Yun and Paul Hattaway, "*The Heavenly Man: The Remarkable True Story of Chinese Christian Brother Yun* (Kregel Publications, 2002)
9. John Piper, I'm Too Distracted With Life To Meditate On Christ, Interview With John Piper, Desiring God, Episode 1762, March 28, 2022,
10. Ruth Chou Simons, *Beholding and Becoming: The Art of Everyday Worship*,152.
11. Ruth Chou Simons, *Beholding and Becoming: The Art of Everyday Worship*,152.
12. Ruth Chou Simons, *Beholding and Becoming: The Art of Everyday Worship*,152.
13. Spurgeon's Sermons (Spokane, Washington; Olive Tree Bible Software; 2010) eBook. Vol. 45, Sermon No. 2644; Titled: The Last Words of Christ on the Cross; Delivered on Lord's Day Evening, June 25th, 1882.
14. Dane Ortlund, *Deeper: Real Change For Real Sinners* (Wheaton:Crossway, 2021),21, E-book.
15. Dane Ortlund, *Deeper: Real Change For Real Sinners*, 23.
16. C.S. Lewis, *The Chronicles of Narnia: The Last Battle* (Harper Collins E-books, 2010) 179.

QUESTIONS FOR PERSONAL REFLECTION OR GROUP DISCUSSION

1. Lois Tverberg, "What Was The 'Good Portion' That Mary Chose?," Our Rabbi Jesus: Insights from Lois Tverberg, September 4, 2012, Accessed May 7, 2022, https://ourrabbijesus.com/articles/what-was-the-good-portion-that-mary-chose/.

Acknowledgments

MOM, YOU ARE BEAUTY PERSONIFIED. THANK YOU FOR YOUR TIRELESS SUPPORT AND FOR TURNING THIS JOURNAL INTO A MASTERPIECE. YOUR ART IS LOVELY. YOUR HEART IS LOVELIER. IF THE WALLS OF THE WORLD COULD BE DECORATED LIKE THE WALLS OF YOUR HEART, WE'D ALL GET A GLIMPSE OF HEAVEN'S SPLENDOR. I WANT TO BE YOU WHEN I GROW UP. I COULDN'T ASK FOR A BETTER TEAMMATE. I LOVE YOU!

KATHY, NOT ONLY DO YOU HAVE MAD GRAMMAR SKILLS, YOU HAVE BEEN THE HANDS AND FEET OF CHRIST TO ME FOR YEARS. WITHOUT THE STEADFASTNESS OF YOUR PRAYERS AND ENCOURAGEMENT, THIS BOOK NEVER WOULD HAVE ENTERED MY MIND. THANK YOU! THANK YOU! THANK YOU!! FOR THE HOURS YOU LABORED IN GENTLY CORRECTING MY MANY ERRORS, AND FOR YOUR DEEPER CONCERN FOR THE CONDITION OF MY HEART. I LOVE YOU!

CHERIE, YOU ARE THE BOMB. WHAT WOULD I DO WITHOUT THE PLEASURE OF YOUR COMPANY, YOUR HOMEMADE ESPRESSO, AND YOUR WILLINGNESS TO WATCH MY KIDDOS SO THAT I COULD HAVE A FEW, UNDISTRACTED HOURS OF WORK EACH WEEK!? YOU ARE THE BEST SISTER THAT EVER WAS A SISTER AND I LOVE YOU SO MUCH!

KYLE, THANK YOU FOR PUTTING UP WITH THE EVER-INCREASING PILES OF LAUNDRY AS I SACRIFICED MATCHED SOCKS TO WRITE THIS BOOK. YOU ARE A WONDERFUL HUSBAND, FATHER, AND THE INSPIRATION FOR SO MUCH OF THIS BOOK. LOVE YOU FOREVER!

LAUNCH TEAM, I AM NOT QUITE SURE HOW I BECAME SO BLESSED WITH SO MANY WONDERFUL SISTERS IN CHRIST. I HAVE BEEN BLOWN AWAY BY YOUR SUPPORT, YOUR ENTHUSIASM, AND YOUR WILLINGNESS TO COME ALONGSIDE ME IN THIS WORK. YOUR IDEAS ARE BRILLIANT, AND YOUR ENCOURAGEMENT HAS KEPT ME GOING. I OWE ALL OF YOU MORE THAN I WILL EVER BE ABLE TO REPAY!

GRANDPAP, THANK YOU FOR NOT COMPLAINING ABOUT MY PILES OF REFERENCE BOOKS ON THE DINING ROOM TABLE, AND MY PROJECTOR SET UP IN YOUR FAVORITE CHAIR. YOUR ENCOURAGEMENT HELPED ME TO PUSH HARD TOWARD THE GOAL! I LOVE YOU SO MUCH!

DAD, THANK YOU FOR THE PRAYERS WHICH HAVE SUPPORTED AND STRUCTURED MY LIFE FROM THE MOMENT I WAS BORN. I DON'T KNOW WHO I WOULD BE WITHOUT THE CONSTANT COVERING OF YOUR INTERCESSION. THANK YOU FOR YOUR FAITHFUL LOVE. I LOVE YOU!

www.ingramcontent.com/pod-product-compliance
Lightning Source LLC
Chambersburg PA
CBHW081708100526
44590CB00022B/3702